IT'S O.K. TO LOVE YOUR CAR™

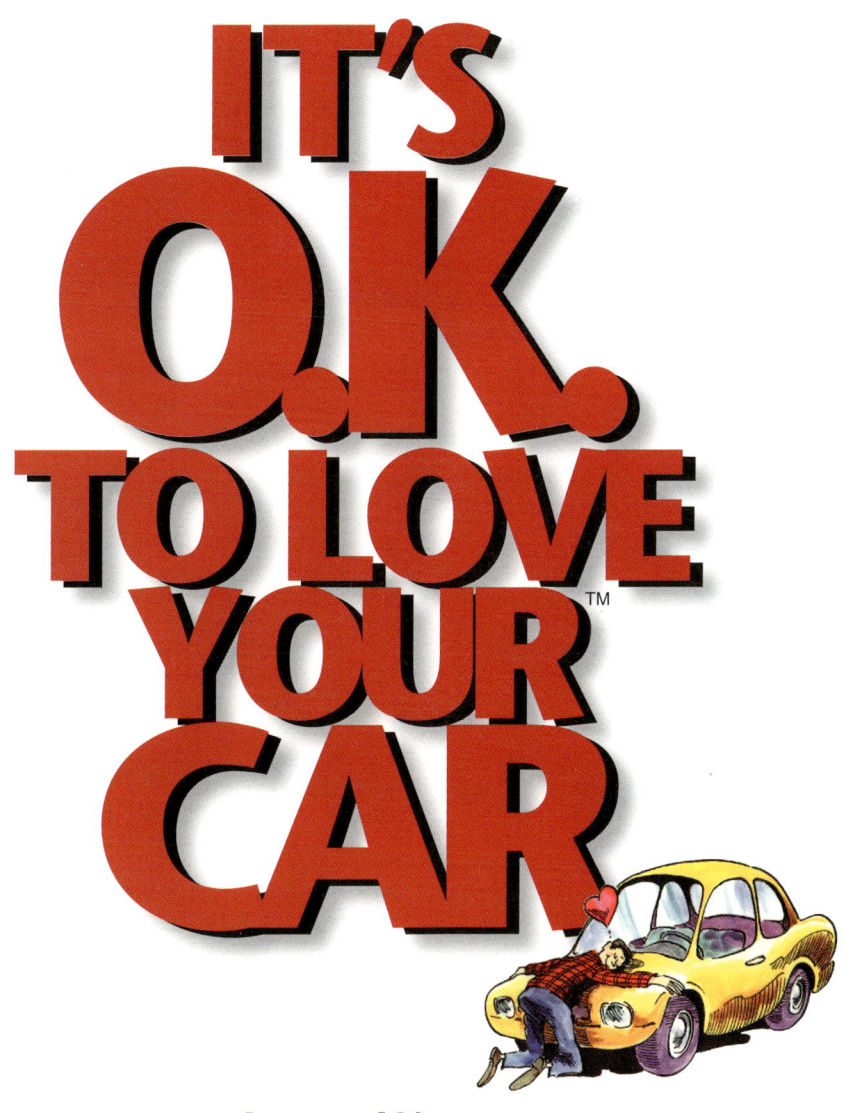

LIVING WITH AUTO EROTIC DEPENDENCY (AED)

Ken Kamstra

Illustrations by Jack Lindstrom
Book design by Ron Long

THE IDEA SHELF

Original Edition
Published by The Idea Shelf, Inc., St.Paul, MN

It's O.K. To Love Your Car
Living With Auto Erotic Dependency (AED)
By Kenneth M. Kamstra

Published by :
The Idea Shelf, Inc.
Two Montcalm Hill
St. Paul, Minnesota 55116

© Copyright 2000 by Kenneth M. Kamstra

Original Edition

Printed in the United States of America

All rights reserved. No part of this book may be reproduced or transmitted in any form or by any means, electronic or mechanical, including photocopying, recording or by any information storage and retrieval system without written permission from the author, except for the inclusion of brief quotations in a review.

This book is designed to provide information in regard to the subject matter covered. Every effort has been made to make it as complete and as accurate as possible. However, there may be mistakes both typographical and in content. The purpose of this book is to educate and entertain. The author and The Idea Shelf, Inc. shall have neither liability nor responsibility to any person or entity with respect to any loss or damage caused, or alleged to be caused, directly or indirectly by the information contained in this book.

The terms "Cargoyle", "Carmudgeon" and "It's O.K. to Love Your" are trademarks of Ken Kamstra.

Publisher's Cataloging-in-Publication
   (Provided by Quality Books, Inc.)

Kamstra, Kenneth M.
    It's OK to love your car : living with auto
  erotic dependency (AED) / by Kenneth M. Kamstra.
  -- 1st ed.
    p. cm.
    LCCN: 99-94328
    ISBN: 0-9671640-0-1

   1. Automobiles--Social aspects--United States.
   2. Automobile ownership--Psychological aspects.
   3. Automobile ownership--Anecdotes.   I. Title.

HE5623.K36 1999   303.4'832
                     QBI99-1341

Contents

About The Author	4
Foreword	6
Acknowledgments	7
1. Why You Love Your Car And Why It Really Is Okay	8
2. Auto Erotic Dependency, AED; You'll Know When You've Got It	14
3. Dad Hated Cars But He Taught Me About Driving	20
4. Higher Learning, Higher Yearning	32
Kewbash Cargoyle	40
5. Bathrooms, The Place For Some Of Your Best Thinking	42
6. Hard Hat Lessons On The Realities Of Life	48
7. Where Have All the Menfolk Gone	58
Assyd Cargoyle	60
8. Learning Mechanics And Manhood The Hard Way	64
9. Freedom Isn't Freedom Unless You Have A Car	72
10. An AED's Ultimate Dilemma: Win A Bride, Surrender A Car	76
11. Learn to Drive And There Are No Limits	82
Suckloot Cargoyle	86
12. Life Skills Taught Here	92
13. The Winds Of Change; An Interview With Eleanor	102
Frenzalong Cargoyle	106
14. "Free Range" Forever; Roads To Riches	108
15. A Suite At The Waldorf	116
16. How The "Golden Ox" Became The Golden Goose	130
17. Does God Hate Porsches?	138
18. The Unpampered Porsche	142
19. Parking Paranoia: Terror In The Buff	152
Keeweenie Cargoyle	154
20. Joe Livinhei; Still Out There Somewhere, Everywhere	158
21. Race Track Driving; It Clears The Mind	166
22. Your Car; More Sinned Against Than Sinner	172
Bad Barf Cargoyle	178
23. The Coming Invasion Of Cargoyles; How It All Began	184
Gotcha Cargoyle	186
24. The Great Silver Bimmer vs. The "Gotcha Cargoyle"	192
25. Up Your Tailpipe; The Smell Of Auto Oblivion	204
Snifferous Cargoyle	206
26. "Steeroids" Launch the Microchip Millennium	210
Gigatrol Cargoyle	214
Epilogue: Driving Enriches Life Even If You Don't Dig Cars	220

About The Author

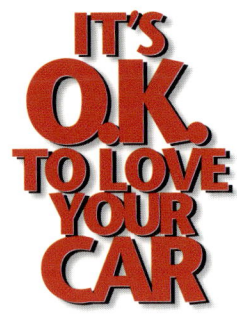

Ken Kamstra calls this his "auto autobiography". In it, he chronicles his passion for driving his own life dreams and the cars that enhanced these driving ambitions. He believes with all his heart that it's okay for you to love your car; and do it without ecological guilt. He is a lifelong car addict, afflicted since childhood with *Auto Erotic Dependency*, AED. Ken has loved every minute of it; and wouldn't cure the addiction if he could. He warns, however, of a worldwide "anti-car conspiracy" that would both shame and legislate an end to cars as we know them; and, of course, to auto enthusiasts.

The author spent his early childhood in western South Dakota's ranch country; but never learned to ride a horse. Instead, he watched, enthralled, as his six older brothers experimented with the "semi-mechanization" of the Kamstra farmstead. Highlight of the process was the reincarnation of a flattened Model T Ford, left for dead under a storm-leveled barn. From his first wild ride on board that skeletal Ford, he knew he was hooked; destined to live – enjoy, actually – life as a car addict. His love of driving extends to his personal life, including the creation of a successful ad agency and other "Kamstra Enterprises".

He is convinced that he is one of the fortunate few born with AED. Most people carry only the Auto Immune Gene, making them largely immune to any real affection for cars or other vehicles. This a-car-is-a-car-is-a-car majority hold most of the world's seats of power and, Kamstra believes, target cars for the abuse of that power.

Kamstra, a journalist-turned-adman, takes a jaundiced view of how the problem began; how it grew; and, most importantly, how you can deal with it. The author's interview with Eleanor Roosevelt – decades ago during his "cheap used car era"– gave him the first, and first hand, clue that "Big Brother" government would be intruding into everyone's life. This intrusion would manifest itself most painfully and personally to anyone who loves cars. In this book, he identifies these diabolically relentless anti-car forces.

Mostly, though, he celebrates the joy that driving brings to life.

With a mix of humor and cynicism – and not always at legal speeds – Kamstra takes you through the highways and backroads of America. It begins with the Model T days on the farm. It spans the "glory days" before the oppressive 55-mile-per-hour national speed limit, emission controls, "gas guzzler" taxes and other Nanny Nation movements. While he has "dabbled" in race track driving and rallying, the author concentrates on "unstructured" auto enjoyment.

From his first car, a 1934 Ford, to his current collection of cars led by a trooper-teasing red Ferrari, Kamstra continues his own "unstructured" auto enthusiasm and encourages every driver to follow suit. The anti-car forces are conjuring up new laws and schemes daily. It's later than you think.

The author and his "ultimate wheels": a 1990 Ferrari Mondial T Cabriolet. A gift to himself for three-plus decades of hard driving.

Foreword

Driving myself and my cars

Your government, always in search of some sense of purpose, continues to lay a massive guilt trip on you and your car. Al Gore, vice president and self appointed leader of the world's environmental doom squads, says that what our vehicles are doing to the environment is "more deadly than any military enemy." His book, "Earth In The Balance", calls for a global program that would "completely eliminate" the internal combustion engine.

If you are one of the multi-zillion majority – the Auto Immune – this assault on your vehicle is no big deal. Should the environmental socialists demand that you switch to an electric car or take the bus, you gladly do it. What do you care so long as you can get from Point A to Point B. Why you'd even give up your SUV to be a better citizen.

Some of us, however, are afflicted with AED, Auto Erotic Dependency. We love our cars. Actually have an emotional involvement with them. Worse, there is no known cure for AED. But you can learn to live with the disease. Yet, if you are willing to make the effort, you can live guilt-free and your life will actually be enriched by AED. This book can help you.

First, you must believe that "It's Okay To Love Your Car". You need have no pangs of conscience no matter what Al Gore or anyone says.

I am one of the endangered species of car lovers. I first became aware of my affliction when Model T Fords still roamed the earth. Duesenbergs, Packards, Cadillacs and other great cars did too, but they came nowhere near the farm where I grew up.

This book is one man's account of a full and rewarding life in spite of – and perhaps because of – his AED disease. Even in the early stages, I also found that I was driving myself as hard as I drove my cars. This may be still another manifestation of the AED Syndrome. Maybe not. All I know is that I was able to drive myself from penniless, high-school-drop-out-poverty to entrepreneurial success.

This book doesn't promise success. It can help you to guilt free peace of mind about your auto enthusiasm.

ACKNOWLEDGMENTS

This book is dedicated mostly to my wife, Mimi, who has managed so well for so long to share me – and, more importantly, the family budget – with my never-ending "auto affairs". I knew when I met her that she was definitely an "Auto Immune" and would never share my love for cars. She had other attributes, however, that more than offset this unfortunate genetic deficiency.

Acknowledgment and apologies are also due my daughters, Linda and Angela, who had to tolerate being stuffed into the back of tiny sports cars while their friends were transported to school in roomy station wagons.

Special appreciation goes to two artists who have helped to bring this book into being. Ron Long, a fellow AED addict, provided design as well as advice; Jack Lindstrom brought each "Cargoyle" to life because he believes as I do that they really exist.

To every reader who has ever made room in his or her heart for a special car, truck, motorcycle or other motorized conveyance, I salute you. AED makes life a little more fun, doesn't it?

CHAPTER 1

WHY YOU LOVE YOUR CAR
AND WHY IT REALLY IS OKAY

Certain genetic research findings have come into my possession. This enlightening data – combined with my own extensive personal experiences and observations – contributes significantly to this book. I confess that, enjoying cars and car people as intensely as I do, I have been guilty of delaying this not inconsiderable undertaking. In other words, this book is long overdue. Acknowledging some immodesty, I believe this book will provide new insights into – and suggested relief for – the mounting social tensions in our land. I believe this to be true even if you don't give a fiddler's damn about cars.

The research to which I refer is that of geneticist Dr. Erhart Von Geernoggin. Working exhaustively with human chromosome structure, Dr. Von Geernoggin came upon a startling discovery. As the story goes, the good doctor was ecstatic.

"Zis cannot be!" he exclaimed. "Cars haff hardly been invented yet!"

Dr. Erhart Von Geernoggin, discoverer of the Auto Erotic Gene.

Exacting scientist that he was, Dr. Von Geernoggin repeated his DNA experiments over and over again. Always the results were the same. The genetic evidence was undeniable.

Certain people – fewer than one in every one hundred – were indeed born with a rare additional gene: the A.E. or *Auto Erotic Gene.* This gene would trigger a powerful emotional response to cars; a response beyond the control of the rational side of the brain. Those possessing this rare gene would be destined to actually become emotionally involved with vehicles that caught their fancy. This involvement would manifest itself in many ways. Carriers of the gene could be expected to spend inordinate amounts of time and energy – not to mention money – bestowing affection on their favorite vehicle or even several vehicles.

Auto Erotic Dependency identified

Dr. Geernoggin, publishing his findings in prestigious medical journals of his time, named the syndrome *Auto Erotic Dependency* or AED. It was a milestone breakthrough in genetic research.

"Zey will be recognized as zee Auto Erotic ones, " Dr. Von Geernoggin remarked to a colleague one day. "Zose vithout zis gene, I call zem the *Auto Immune*. Zey vill be able to take cars or leef zem alone. Pragmatic people but never passionate."

The Auto Immune, he explained, are the norm. Their lives will be more well ordered, uncomplicated, uninteresting.

"Zee Auto Erotic ones – zey vill haff one hell ov a lot more fun," Dr. Von Geernoggin chuckled to himself one night as he locked up his laboratory.

Colleagues had little interest in Dr. Von Geernoggin's work or his opinions. They were among the Auto Immune and had only scorn for what they considered his lunacy. The doctor spent most of his time alone in later life. The year was l891. A few "horseless carriages" were being tinkered with by inventors, but no one believed the horse could ever be replaced.

Thus, the world paid little heed to Dr. Von Geernoggin. He died in obscurity without receiving the recognition he so richly deserved for his pioneering efforts. He was shunned by the very Auto Immune multitudes his research had identified.

In some small way, this book will attempt to atone for this affront to the visionary genius of the late Dr. Von Geernoggin. I, for one, am glad I was born with the A.E. Gene he isolated. It has been fun, like my first wild ride in a "modified" Model T. It has been frightening as in my first run on a real, balls-to-the-wall race track. It has been frustrating to suffer the scorn and suspicion I get from my Auto Immune friends and neighbors. If only I had come upon Geernoggin's monumental works earlier in life. It would have explained so much of what had been bewildering too me.

Auto Immune identified

Learn to recognize "Cargoyles". These evil, anti-car creatures are out to spoil your driving fun. Don't let them.

A sinister plot was hatched

There was that pretty girl in second grade. She had long blond curls and big blue eyes; and I swear she was flirting with me at recess. I cared not one whit for her charms but was enthralled with her dad's big Buick. He used it on occasion to take some of us farm kids to our one-room school. Then there were the times, after we had moved to town, when I would spend hours at the city junk yard just to sit in old cars and go on pretend tours to far away places. It all made sense when I learned about AED and the Auto Erotic Gene.

You probably have some form of AED, too; otherwise you wouldn't be reading this book.

If Dr. Von Geernoggin had lived in this century, he undoubtedly would have predicted the inevitable clash between the Auto Immune and the Auto Erotic. Even the most seminally Auto Immune could still appreciate the utility value of their cars, of course, but saw them only as four-wheeled appliances.

Cars to the Immune would forever be little more than a device for getting from here to there. As Dr. Von Geernoggin once conjectured: no consuming passion; just convenience. The Auto Immune cannot comprehend a car lover's joyous enthusiasm for his machine. They can, however, detract from that joy. Most often through indifference – but sometimes with malicious intent – they will do bodily injury to your cherished chariot. These hurts are mostly an annoyance but can range upward to a genuinely traumatic experience.

I would carry Dr. Geernoggin's theories one step further. I strongly suspect that the absence of the Auto Erotic Gene is behind the congenital, humorless insecurity and intolerance of many Auto Immune people. Auto Immunes seem to gravitate toward government jobs. From these power positions, they can pass laws not only against cars but against driving ambitions that might precipitate unequal distribution of wealth.

Still, for some decades, we coexisted in relative harmony; the Auto Erotic and the Auto Immune sharing the same streets, the same roads, the same world.

Cars evolved. Cars multiplied to hundreds of millions of vehicles in all sizes, shapes and colors. Freeways criss-crossed America and many other nations.

It might have gone on this way forever.

Neither the car lovers nor the Auto Immune were aware of it, but a sinister plot was being hatched by a few radicals within the Auto Immune majority. Their plot was made all the easier by the indifference of these Auto Immune masses.

First stage in the evil scheme was to lay an ecology-based guilt trip on every motorist everywhere. Turn neighbor against neighbor; wife against hubby; father against son; all this and more in the name of saving our planet. Then, with the motorist masses thus softened and divided, move in for the *coup de grace.* Put an end forever to cars and their infernal internal combustion engines.

I cannot tell you exactly when the conspiracy began or who the original conspirators were. I doubt that anyone really knows. More and more voices – and ever more strident voices – joined in the "cars-will-kill-us-all" chorus. Two were prominent among the early doomsayers. Rachel Carson frightened the daylights out of me and an entire world with her book, "The Silent Spring" (1962). It portrayed a world in which reckless human polluters kill off all the birds while generally making an unlivable mess of the planet.

Even more dire consequences of our callous indifference to Mother Earth were predicted by Paul Ehrlich, a biology professor at Stanford University. His best-selling book, "The Population Bomb" (1968), while railing against too many babies and not enough babying of the earth, took particular aim at automobiles. To him, cars were a major cause of our "race to oblivion."

An obvious Auto Immune, the good doctor advocated electric cars as a "small price to pay" for improved air purity.

An ecology-based guilt trip

Auto Erotics: in danger of becoming an endangered species

Not to be upstaged, Congress created the Environmental Protection Agency with the power to do just about anything to anybody by invoking the word "environment". The word had become the mantra of environmental activists everywhere. Al Gore, then senator, swept himself into the Vice President's office and cleaned up handsomely with royalties on his book, "Earth In The Balance" (1992). Taking up the "sky-is-falling" cudgel, he condemns your car and mine. Even your power lawn mower is suspect.

Could this be true? Are we asphyxiating our fellow citizens just for the sake of our selfish indulgence in cars? Will we have to hang our heads in shame as "global warming" melts the polar ice and drowns us all in a "Water World"? Are birds, bees, trees and even people dying just because of our foolhardy addiction to the internal-combustion-powered automobile?

Are we the environmental enemy?

In a word, no. There are mountains of sound, scientific evidence – compiled over many decades – proving that none of the doomsayers' predictions have come true or have any likelihood of ever happening.

Forget all the hype, hypocrisy and fear mongering. The environment is getting better; not worse. Our old world is still doing what it has always done for millions of years: spinning along into eternity and pretty much taking care of itself as it always has. Our cars – never a serious threat to the environment in the first place – are "exhaling" ever more pure exhaust, getting more miserly with gas and even becoming recyclable. All of us need to help make the world an even better place to live; whether that means tuning our cars, recycling our waste or planting our share of the four million new trees Americans plant every day. We need to help; we don't need to be hysterical.

It's okay to love your car, and it's okay to drive it with a clear conscience. While the good earth keeps on spinning, I suggest you take that car of yours for a spin today. Wherever you live, there are thousands of miles of interesting roads not far away that will take you out into the natural beauty of the countryside. America, not incidentally, is about 98% countryside even with all its roads, towns and cities. In fact, there are fun roads awaiting you just about everywhere in the world.

While you're driving, go ahead and test your skill on some of the tighter curves if you're so inclined, but slow down and enjoy the view as well. Unless you are doing the desert scene, you'll find plenty of trees; America, for instance, has more forests today than it had way back in 1920. Notice the tall corn and the lush fields of grain. We're feeding more people than ever and they're living longer and better than ever in spite of Dr. Ehrlich's 1960's predictions. Global warming? Yes, about 1/2 a degree since 1888 and none since 1940. Listen to the birds. There are billions of them. Apparently none have read Rachel Carson's book. Your library or bookstore has many books that take an honest, objective look at our environment and find little to worry about.

We Auto Erotics are in danger of becoming an endangered species. And do you really think the Endangered Species Act will concern itself with our plight? Hang in there. It is okay to love your car. There is no reason on earth – or above earth in the atmosphere – why you shouldn't continue, even intensify, your enthusiasm for that beautiful, responsive machine you drive. Loving your car, pushing it to its limit, pampering it, polishing it, protecting it, preening in its mirror finish; all are good, healthy car guy or gal activities. What's more, it will help you to rid yourself of the guilt trip being laid on you by car haters.

Car lovers arise! Get rolling! Dr. Von Geernoggin would be pleased.

■ ■ ■

Car lovers arise!

CHAPTER 2

AUTO EROTIC DEPENDENCY, AED; YOU'LL KNOW WHEN YOU'VE GOT IT

I was airborne in the skeletal remains of a Model T Ford when my budding addiction became irreversible. I didn't know what it was, of course, but there was no turning back. I was only seven, yet some of life's decisions come early and they are absolute. I decided that I liked whatever it was that was happening in my psyche. My brother, Hank, was at the wheel and I was hanging on for dear life, trying to keep my bare feet off the red hot exhaust pipe. Hank was seventeen and unquestionably the wildest of the seven Kamstra brothers. Unquestionably, too, he was AED addicted. The disease, however, had not yet been recognized by the medical profession. Hank never drove any other way than flat out. At this instant, it was decision time for him. He had just maneuvered the old Ford – actually just a frame, motor and steering wheel – around a hair-raising turn and was cresting a small rise in the dusty dirt road.

We both saw it at once! There, dead ahead, was a T in the road. Option A: turn sharp right. Option B: take a sharp left. Either option would surely have thrown us from our mount and this story would only have appeared in the weekly funeral notices of the Canby News. Farmers in that part of southwestern Minnesota were always crippling or killing themselves with one damn fool stunt or another. Hank stayed calm – I admired him for that – and assessed his options. With the gas pedal to the floor and no brakes, his only option was straight ahead. Our momentum took us cleanly over the open ditch and we must have cleared the barbed wire fence by a good inch.

We were sure as hell airborne.

■ ■ ■

Neither Henry Ford nor God intended for Model T's to fly, but then you might say it was an act of God that brought us to this exhilarating moment. The Ford – when it had a body and brakes and all – was the Kamstra's go-to-town-Saturday car. I doubt that anyone in the family knew or cared what vintage Model T it was when Dad traded it for some livestock a few years earlier. I would guess maybe 1923 or 24. To my young eyes, it was a grand limousine, side curtains and all, as it carried 6 or 8 of the 11 Kamstra sons and daughters still living on the farm. Dad never trusted that Ford or any motorized vehicle for that matter.

"Horses are a damned site more reliable," he used to say to anyone who would listen. Horses he knew from back in the days when he drove wagon trains through the mountains of Oregon.

Dad never quite got the hang of driving cars.

Then God, or at least the forces of nature, stepped in one hot summer's night with a terrible windstorm that flattened our barn and the Ford with it. Looking back, I suspect that Dad was happy to be rid of the darned thing.

Hank, on the other hand, saw it as an opportunity, pure and simple. With the help of some of my older brothers – I had six of them – they dragged the remains of the Ford out from under the barn and began to resurrect it. The body was deemed unsalvageable but also non essential. I watched every minute of the process like an intern seeing surgery for the first time.

Little did I know that – in the recesses of my unspoiled, uncomplicated country bumpkin brain – lifetime attitudes were being etched into the gray matter. I would forever more have this passionate love affair with cars, engines and things mechanical. I had Auto Erotic Dependency; no question about it.

A magic carpet to the outside world

Something even more profound was occurring. I was witnessing, first hand, a milestone in the evolution of man from the horse age to the car age. Dad, his heels dug into the horse age, would never believe that horses couldn't do anything that really needed doing. His sons – these callused, improvising surgeons gathered around a comatose Model T – saw the future in the internal combustion engine. The evolution/revolution that centered around this engine actually began before the turn of the century. But now, in this glorious summer of 1933 it had come to our farm. We were dirt poor and coming out of a depression, but, by God, this little four-banger engine was for me a magic carpet to the outside world.

After weeks of tinkering, tweaking and swearing, one day the engine sputtered and popped to life. I heard few engine sounds back then, but this one was a symphony as stirring as the Ferraris that I would one day be privileged to drive. Except for fresh air and freedom, we Kamstra's were strangers to "privilege" at this stage in our lives.

"Get in!" Hank shouted over the roar of the engine. "And hang on!"

Hank may have sensed my awed admiration as I watched him resurrect this seemingly demolished Ford. More likely, his quick insights told him I was the only one dumb enough to join him on the first trial run. In minutes, we were out on the narrow dirt road that connected our farm – the landlord's farm actually – to the rest of Minnesota and the world beyond.

"Whooeeeee!"

I wish you could have begun your car love as I did with one of America's first cars. But, then, you would be older right now than you want to be. Still in all, if you're passionate about full participation in the driving process – not just mindless steering – you have limitless opportunity to experience this addictive euphoria. It is a visceral sensation that overwhelms the senses, penetrating right down to the soul when you are going like a bat out of hell with lots of open road ahead of you. Anthropologists may have insights into why man has always wanted to roam free and go fast. But, then, anthropologists aren't likely to be Auto Erotics, so we may never get to the bottom of it.

All I know is, Hank and I were having one helluva good time roaring over the backroads that day. All roads were "back roads" around our farm, of course. We tried not to miss a single one. That's when we came to the dead end and were instantly airborne. It was a brief but beautiful flight. Three days of rain earlier in the week had softened our landing strip. The Ford came down on all fours – without even blowing a tire – in old Anton Backel's field. We plowed up maybe a hundred feet or so of his prize wheat. Anton would be mad as hell.

Hank and I just looked at each other and grinned. The grins grew into laughter until tears made rivers down our dust-caked faces. Then and there, I knew I wanted to be a car guy when I grew up.

"Whooeeeee!"

■ ■ ■

Cars and engines would play a key role in my life. I didn't know how; I just knew it. I would drop out of high school to buy my first car. The Navy would train me to operate all manner of machinery including beach landing craft; not the cushiest job in war time, but a learning experience. My first journalist's job turned out to be one that most car guys would kill for even if it didn't rate a press club membership. As a roving reporter for South Dakota's Huron Daily Plainsman, my beat was both Dakotas and even a foray into surrounding states If I chose. Imagine. Roaming thousands of miles in a hopped up, dual exhaust Ford V8 just exploring for stories, meeting people, having a ball. Any journalist worth his salt had to master the lumbering Speed Graphlex camera; so I learned. I was the Charles Kuralt of the fifties, minus, of course, the fat salary and the fame. But I was talking to Pony Express riders (retired), rodeo stars, archaeologists recreating ancient Indian villages and not a few celebrities. I even interviewed Eleanor Roosevelt. Charming, but we were miles apart politically. My salary was meager, but my aspirations were not. The specter of a New Deal-government-controlled life, however secure, was repugnant to me. Maybe it was the gut reaction of an addicted driver. Maybe car guys are so fiercely independent because they are drivers in their careers as well as in their cars. I was.

Brother Hank.

Cars: life reference and rejuvenation

The only journalist's jobs I ever coveted were those held down by those lucky stiffs writing for *Car & Driver, Road & Track, Automobile* and other great "car books". I console myself with the knowledge that my own writing, idea-generating career would come to afford me many of the cars that these guys just write about. Many of these cars, from the late sixties on, sit pristinely and patiently in my garage waiting their turn at another back roads blast. A fleeting return to their youth and mine. Year upon year, decade after decade, cars have always been a reference point in my life. They haven't overshadowed the good people and the good times; they just help bring the memories back to life and back into the perspective of time.

AED, fortunately as I see it, doesn't get better with time. If anything, it becomes more intense as your leisure time and your bank account grows. What a wonderful, youth-perpetuating disease!

■ ■ ■

From Dragster To "Deputy";
The Second Life Of Mick Kieffer

Dragsters were Mick Kieffer's hobby – actually AED therapy – in his youth. So was just about any other car-related activity he could get his hands on. Skilled hands that designed circuit boards during working hours. After hours, when he wasn't playing with cars, Mick livened parties with his impersonation of "Barney Fife", the bumbling-but-lovable deputy on the early sixties "Andy Griffith Show". Friends thought he not only looked and sounded like Barney but had his every goofy mannerism down pat.

"Barney" with his "Mayberry Cruiser", a get well gift from his wife, Kathy.

Mick's "Barney Thing" might never have gone beyond parties had it not been for a near-terminal illness. Mick, then 47, was diagnosed with "aspergillosis", an often-fatal lung disease. Doctors at Minnesota's Mayo Clinic, advised Mick and his wife, Kathy, to go home and "get their lives in order".

They did in a way. Wife, Kathy, a capable car buff in her own right, found just the car to welcome Mick home. It was a 1963 Ford Galaxy. "Barney's" police cruiser. Not the real one, but a look-alike by the time Kathy and family and friends "restored" it complete with "Mayberry Police" door badge, big red light on top. The works.

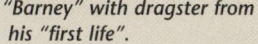

Frail after 45 days of surgery and intensive care, Barney began his "second life" as Barney Fife impersonator; complete with patrol car. Mick didn't say so, but I believe this is a case where a car was recovery therapy as well as AED therapy.

"Barney" with dragster from his "first life".

Mick soon hit the road nationally with his "Spirit of Mayberry" Show. Car shows are a mainstay of his bookings, but they also include FBI gatherings, Conventions, 911 seminars and even weddings. At weddings, the bride and groom find themselves "booked" and handcuffed together. "Barney" loves to hand out badges to "deputize" children. He swears them in but cautions them, "no actual swearing".

Is Mick's second life a success? Well, you have to book his show at least a year in advance.

Kids love "Barney" as he swears them in with a "no swearing" oath.

CHAPTER 3

Dad Hated Cars But He Taught Me About Driving

"Everything must go."

They started coming right after sunup that morning. The scavengers. The bargain hunters. The curious. A few plodded onto our farmyard with wagon and team. Most came by truck or by car. All were prepared to carry away their booty.

The Kamstras were quitting farming; selling out to pay off delinquent bank loans. Martin Kamstra's 35-year farming venture was ending. but his hard-driving lessons would live on in his children.

The sun bathed our farm in the warmth of an early autumn in southwestern Minnesota farm country. Green apples and orange red plums hung heavy from the trees in our orchard; fruit that mom canned to help us through the long winters. At least the sun would help to dispel some of the gloom and finality of the unfolding events this day. September 19, 1936. The end of a farming career sustained by the sweat and determination of Martin and Annie Kamstra – and children – since their marriage in 1902.

I stayed in the house longer than usual this morning, alternately watching Dad and Mom at the breakfast table and the events outside. At 10, I didn't understand the economics of farming or of life itself for that matter. I knew only that we were about to surrender all our worldly goods, the stuff that made our close-knit farm life possible. Everything would be fair game to the auctioneer's unintelligible but persuasive spiel.

Just outside the kitchen window, defiant and proud in its nakedness, stood the resurrected Model T that had awakened my Auto Erotic Gene. We had saved it from the wrath of a summer storm; we couldn't save it from the auctioneer's block. Bank foreclosure rules say, "everything must go."

It was a sad day for me. It must have been devastating for Mom and Dad. They sat at the kitchen table drinking still another cup of coffee as they watched the buyers and gawkers arrive. Over the decades of their farm life, coffee was essential. It always began at daybreak when Dad would stoke up the wood-burning kitchen stove. Countless hours, I had watched him wield his razor-sharp ax to split new wood, always miraculously missing his fingers by fractions of an inch. Next he would add a generous amount of ground coffee to the enamel pot that had seen almost as many farm mornings as he had. Soon, the drafty old kitchen would be cozy warm; a pleasure heightened by the smell of Dad's "special brew" drifting all through the house.

Mom warranted the privilege – she knew few privileges in her life – of being served the first cup in bed. It was a ritual from which they never varied. Looking down on them as they sipped their first cup each morning was their ornately framed wedding portrait. They were a handsome young couple and the permanence of their marriage vows was something that neither of them would ever question. Theirs was not a "relationship"; it was a "till death do us part" marriage.

Perhaps this morning's coffee didn't taste as sweet as usual, even with the two spoons of sugar plus cream. Neither of them spoke.

Dad wasn't physically imposing. A couple inches shy of six feet, he probably weighed in at about 165. Back in 1876, when Dad was born, his height was about normal. Neither tall nor broad shouldered, Dad was, nonetheless hard as nails. A lifetime of physical toil showed in his weathered face and callused hands. His heavy mustache belonged on his face as did the grizzled stubble of beard. The stubble was shaved clean – with his trusty straight edged razor – once or twice a week. Dad was truly a man of the soil and of endless toil. He was 60.

Mom, at 58, had lost her youthful figure. She was now "heavy" as she preferred to describe herself. The pretty face was still there. There, too, was the loving and compassionate disposition that must have helped her weather a lifetime of raising eleven children. Her twin daughters died of "summer complaint" at six months. Had they lived, ours would have been a family of thirteen children and Mom and Dad would have found room in their hearts and their home for little Ollie and Annie too.

Dad was hard as nails

And then all the banks closed

The sun was higher now. It bounced off the gleaming finishes that set apart the new cars driven by some of the more affluent neighbors. Without question, this would be an intensely painful humiliation for Dad and Mom. Once they had been the farmers whose success was the envy of many other farmers in the counties of eastern South Dakota. Most neighboring farmers coveted Dad's corn. Somehow, it always stood higher and looked healthier than most any other corn in the county. From these bountiful yields and that of other cash crops, the Kamstras of that happy era had clothes, "grocery money" and could even throw a party now and then.

But that was many years ago. Amidst this plenty, Dad was somehow persuaded that moving west to Missouri River country would be even more fruitful. It was a mistake from which they never recovered no matter how many hours a day they worked, no matter how much they sacrificed. The soil on their farm near Pierre, South Dakota, was rock hard, dry and unproductive.

It would get much worse.

Drought would parch the land, killing or stunting the growth of the few crops that managed to break through the soil. Dad went deeply into debt trying to make his farming venture a success.

Then, on Friday, October 28, 1929, "Black Friday" happened! The U.S. stock exchange collapsed and with it America's economy and that of most of the rest of the world. The Kamstra's had no money in the stock market, of course, but Dad and some of my older brothers did have meager savings in the bank. Small accounts, only a few hundred dollars, but enough to give them some measure of accomplishment for all their dawn-to-dusk labor.

And then all the banks closed! They succumbed to the incessant demands of depositors panicked by what history would record as "The Great Depression".

All Dad and the family knew was that their meager savings were gone. Bank doors in Pierre were locked and no amount of pounding or pleading would open them. Promises were made that the banks would soon reopen and repay their depositors, but in his heart, Dad knew it would not happen. It didn't.

The Kamstra family was learning, first hand, what was meant by the term "dirt poor". I was just a toddler then; my older brothers and sisters experienced this phase of our lives more vividly and painfully. Still, even at age three, I sensed the hardships we were enduring. I was aware of roadside fence posts nearly buried in powder-fine dust; dust that at times seemed to blot out the sun and turn day into night when the wind blew.

And the wind blew often, carrying with it the tumbleweeds. The song "Tumbling Tumble Weeds" popularized this phenomenon of the parched prairie, made it somehow seem romantic. It wasn't. The "damned tumble weeds", as Dad called them, were only good to provide fuel for the pot bellied parlor furnace that heated our house. I joined the older Kamstra kids to collect them. A more stable and longer burning fuel was a well dried "cow pie". We collected them too. Every day we made the rounds, bare feet slapping on the hard surface of the fields. Every day, Dad and Mom would pray for rain – prayers preceded every meal – before anyone was permitted to start on breakfast.

Their prayers went unanswered. With an irony that must have seemed tinged with cruelty for Dad and Mom, the most popular song of the day was "Singing In The Rain".

Then the grasshoppers came; hordes of grasshoppers!

They devoured whatever the sun and wind hadn't already killed. There wasn't anything my parents or any of the ten Kamstra brothers and sisters still at home could do but hope that someday their prayers would be answered. Making the best of things, Dad sent the scrawny Kamstra kids out into the fields with buckets of water. No, the water wasn't to save the crops ; our mission was to

"damned tumble weeds"

catch grasshoppers – there were millions of them – and throw them into the water buckets. The water kept them from jumping out until we could get them back to the farmyard. There they became "cost free" chicken feed. Eggs were an occasional treat on the farm but not an everyday diet staple. Eggs, after all, were also a "cash crop" as was milk from the cows and even the chickens themselves. Killing a chicken for food or butchering a farm animal for meat made possible an occasional feast. But each bird or beast eaten was one less producer of marketable farm produce.

■ ■ ■

Dad and Mom were undoubtedly reflecting on all this as the time for the auction's start approached. Somehow, they had survived those years of farming and ranching in western South Dakota and had made their way, ultimately, to this "final farm" in southwestern Minnesota.

Our farm life would come to an end this day in September. I had no perspective against which to measure this life vs. another, but I was sure I would miss it for the most part. To me, it had meant acres of fields and valleys and streams to explore with my sisters, Jean and Phyllis. Too young to be of much use in the fields, we were still allowed the luxury of being kids. Older brothers had farm work to do or had moved away along with my older sisters to start lives apart from the Kamstra farmstead.

One facet of farm life I wouldn't miss at all: walking six miles to and from school in winter. To school meant heading north into the wind. "Wind-chill" temperatures hadn't been popularized then, but often they must have fallen to 50 or more below zero. It was brutal for a seven year old. I pleaded with my brother, Leslie , to "please let me go back!" but he would refuse. Six years older than me, he knew that I would have frozen to death before I ever made it back to the warm sanctuary of Mom's kitchen. On some days – I don't know how or why these days were chosen – we were taken to school by neighbors who could provide conveyances. I will always remember the "sleigh" that one farmer chose to transport us to school. Actually, it was a manure spreader wagon box with its four wheels replaced by sleigh runners. We all huddled under cowhide robes inside the wagon box, sharing the warmth of our body heat as the sleigh bumped and groaned over the frozen country roads. Inevitably before we reached the school, the heat from our young bodies began to "reactivate" the frozen manure liberally caked inside the wagon box.

The stink became increasingly nauseating as the manure thawed, but it was not nearly as hard to take as walking or being dragged to school.

Homeward bound at the end of the day was almost always easier. The wind was usually at our backs and, besides, Mom would probably have something good cooking or baking in the kitchen. The Kamstras were still poor but Mom knew how to stretch a meager budget. My favorite was something called "pigs in blankets", pork sausage rolled in dough, then into the oven where they would be baked to a golden brown. Smelling them and seeing them come out of the oven made everything right in my limited little world. Pigs in blankets almost made up for "lard bread" days. We complained but in our hearts we really knew it was the best that Mom's resources would allow on those days. And so we ate slices of bread spread with lard over which we poured syrup to hide the taste.

The cook stove and furniture would at least be spared from the auction block. Next to our beds and the "parlor furnace" in the living/dining room, I would vote the cook stove as the most important household furnishing we owned. After supper, we all sat around the radio. Television hadn't been invented and we couldn't afford a telephone, so there was little else to distract us. "Jack Armstrong The All American Boy" was my favorite radio hero. And at age

> *The heat began to "reactivate" the frozen manure*

ten, I fell head over heels in love with Shirley Temple, mostly from staring at her likeness in the bottom of my cereal bowl.

Some two decades later, I would meet her in San Francisco while doing interviews for a commercial film. But the magic was gone. She was married and putting on weight and so was I.

"We did our best"

■ ■ ■

This day, however, I was still totally innocent of any goings on in the world outside the Kamstra farm and a few miles beyond. Dad finally finished his last cup of coffee. He rose from the kitchen table. Mom was still sitting. He squeezed her hand inside his gnarled hand and said, "well, Mum," and turned to leave.

I expected him to make a more dramatic pronouncement, but Annie Kamstra knew exactly what her husband was saying. "We did our best."

I followed Dad out to the yard, the sun warm on my face. It felt good, comforting. Yet the air was ominously still and heavy. It was a day like the one just three years before when a tornado descended on us smashing our barn, killing some livestock and moving on in an instant while we all watched in terror. Now, at least, there was a brand new barn, courtesy of The Farmers Insurance Company.

City Dwellers. After a lifetime of farming, and then losing it all, Martin and Annie Kamstra finally relax. Their's was an era when "horse power" was actually provided by horses.

The bright red barn paint was intensified by the morning sun as the farmers gathered in front of it, eager for the action to start. They would not have long to wait. Clayton South, the auctioneer, was making his way to the platform that had been erected for the sale. From his elevated perch, he would hold court like the high priest of property redistribution. The sale would probably go on until well into the afternoon. Throughout southwestern Minnesota and even into South Dakota and Iowa, Clayton South was affectionately known as "South the mouth". He did know his calling. He had the auctioneer's banter, lingo and crowd-pleasing bid parlance down to a fine art.

I didn't share their affection for him. To me, he was just a fat slob come to put an end to my dad's lifetime endeavor. Clayton was short, maybe five six at most. He tried to compensate with a high-standing western hat and high heeled cowboy boots. His expensive western shirt – with pearl snaps instead of buttons – completed the get up. In spite of its obvious quality construction, the shirt could not fully contain Clayton's enormous belly. It hung over his belt, hiding the hand tooled silver buckle that somehow kept the belt from giving way.

After a little friendly joshing to warm up the crowd, Clayton began. To open the sale , he had selected an item he thought would have near universal appeal. It was a hand-held, one-horse plow of the kind depicted in state seals that tend to glorify the pioneering farmer.

Classic plow, cursed tractor

"Aw right, what am I bid for this genuine hand plow…a collectors item, folks, a jen-yoo-wine collectors item that will be worth real money some day! You don't hardly see them no more. Do I hear…"

The rapid fire, sing-song staccato droned on. Looking at the plow with its decades-worn handles and still shiny blade, I remembered walking behind Dad as he forced the blade into the soil. The reins were draped around Dad's neck while he urged the horse forward and skillfully turned over row upon row of fresh black soil. It was a treat for a young boy's bare feet…and for his soul. Birds seemed to come from everywhere to feast on the worms and bugs as the plow exposed them.

In minutes the handsome plow was gone. Sold! "Everything must go!" Clayton kept saying as the farmers continued bidding and competing with one another. They seemed not to care how rickety or rusty a piece of machinery was; if they could get it cheap, they wanted it. The old gray Fordson Tractor was probably approaching collectors item status, too, but Clayton chose not to glorify it. He had fun with it, joking about the big fat gas tank that straddled the engine and the giant steel wheels that were a little bowed from too many years in service. My oldest brother, Lewis, the unofficial mechanic of the family, had no fun at all with the old Fordson. There was hardly a day that went by that he didn't curse this old tractor, the Ford Motor Company and old Henry

Ford himself. More often than not, Louie's stream of profanity would pour out from under the tractor where Louie lay, grease covered and sprawled among his tools. But it was a tractor, more or less, and it was the closest the Kamstra farming operation would ever come to mechanization.

When the Fordson was sold – its final humiliation to go for $45 – Louie pretended an attitude of "good riddance" but truth was that he and that cantankerous old beast had developed a kind of adversarial but warm relationship. As the new owner chugged away with the Fordson – for him it started on the first try – it would leave a certain vacuum in Louie's life from this day forward.

I tuned out much of the strange dialog between Clayton and the crowd. Then our old cultivator came on the block. That got my attention.

"God!", I thought, "I will I be glad to see that cultivator go."

For more than a year, embarrassment and shame came flooding over me every time I saw that cursed cultivator. It was even worse when I watched one of my older brothers skillfully maneuver it out into the field in easy command of the two horse team that pulled it.

I had failed "the rites of manhood" on that damned machine. I was nine when it happened. Dad was pulling into our driveway after a day of cultivating. Seeing me, he stopped the rig and motioned me over. Before I knew it, he was hoisting me into the driver's seat.

"Take 'em to the barn," he said as he handed me the reins.

I couldn't have been more thrilled if the rig had been a Roman chariot and this was to be my first race.

"Dad thinks I'm ready to be a man," I said to myself as the leather of the reins was firmly in my hands. Unabashed pride welled up inside me. So did fear.

> **I had failed "the rites of manhood"**

The horses immediately sensed the fear.

"Giddyup!" I said in the most commanding voice I could muster.

The team lurched forward. First they trotted and then went to a full run. A runaway! Midway across our yard – with Dad and two older brothers running and yelling after me – the cultivator hit a rock on the downward slope toward our barn. The impact bounced me out of the driver's seat and I was now spread eagle across the rig, hanging on for dear life.

Brother, Leslie, the fastest runner, managed to grab the bridle of one of the horses and pull them to a stop. My rescuers undoubtedly suppressed an urge to chew my ass for losing control of the team and for bending the wheel of our one-and-only cultivator.

I stood there, knees trembling, nose bleeding, trying through a fat bloody lip to convince them it was all the horses' fault. My pride hurt worse than anything and I wasn't going to add to my humiliation. I would not cry no matter what! Soon, everyone forgot the incident.

I never did. It convinced me that I was a car guy and machine guy and not a horses guy.

■ ■ ■

Auto Immunes... every damn one

My reactions ranged from indifference to outright boredom as the auction droned on into late afternoon. The sun, once warm and comforting to me, was now just plain hot. Clayton was sweating more profusely than ever. He kept a thick towel rolled around the back of his neck to soak up some of the sweat. But Clayton never lost enthusiasm for his work and seemed to enjoy the commanding resonance of his own voice. "Sevny sevny sevny sevny…do I hear sevny fi…sevny fi…", and on and on. He was auctioning off livestock now. No more 5 a.m. milking for the Kamstra males. Nobody would miss that much.

Then Blacky was led into the sales arena. Blacky was the only colt among the four horses we kept on our farm. He was a beautiful colt; his coal black hide shone in the hot sun. The white triangle on his forehead made him even more beautiful in my opinion. And he was friendly. I had helped Dad with the colt's delivery and in appreciation Dad told me the colt would be mine. It was a figure of speech, of course, but I took it to heart. I named him after the "Black Beauty" horse that was the hero of a book read to us by our teacher.

Now fat Clayton was about to auction Blacky off to the highest bidder. Damn! It wasn't Clayton's fault that Blacky had to be sold, of course, but my rage grew. It grew some more when Clayton swaggered to the edge of the auction stage and climbed on Blacky's back. I was sure poor Blacky would buckle under the auctioneer's weight.

"Fat bastard!" I said under my breath .

"Ah'm gonna sell this cute little colt right out from under me," Clayton roared to the crowd as they all laughed at the colt's oversized rider.

Minutes later, good to his word, Clayton had sold Blacky, the "item" on the auctioneer's list: "Gelding Colt, black." Winning bid, $62. Shit!

The Ford, the flying Ford, went for even less: $22. What the hell did these guys know about life or about cars. Auto Immunes, every damn one.

Then it was over; over forever and ever. Martin and Annie Kamstra would never farm again.

When we got back to the house, the radio was blaring with news about the wondrous, "New Deal" accomplishments of Franklin D. Roosevelt since his landslide reelection. Dad was a Democrat of sorts; at least he believed that wealthy people were automatically no good. It was a belief undoubtedly strengthened by the fact that "rich" bankers had kept his money when they closed the banks back in the depression of '29. And now, of course, they were auctioning off his farming possessions; an auction that, ironically, fell $144.78 short of bank debts.

I shared Dad's political convictions well into early adulthood but ultimately switched as I realized government help had little to do with an individual's success or failure. I never discussed this with Dad. After his "retirement", he was the recipient of one of Roosevelt's "New Deal" programs. The Works Progress Administration – WPA – provided him "make work". He never said anything, but it must have been degrading to a once fiercely independent farmer in charge of his own destiny.

Nonetheless, Dad would not have been pleased if he had learned that later in life I would infuriate Eleanor Roosevelt by asking if her husband had a hand in ignoring warnings of impending Japanese attacks on Pearl harbor. At least I was carrying on the Kamstra's "stubborn Dutchman" tradition of tackling issues head on.

Most events from one's youth seem to disappear and dissolve behind you as each new day presents its "tyranny of the immediate". The house where our farming came to an end, however, still stands, empty but defying the passage of time. I go back to reminisce now and then and if I concentrate I can still see Dad taking Mother's hand in his and hear him saying, "Well, Mum." And I see her looking up at him and knowing exactly what he meant. "We did our best."

Do your best. It's a driving lesson taught me by a tough old guy who hated cars but damn well knew what driving was all about.

■ ■ ■

> *He damn well knew what driving was all about*

CHAPTER 4

HIGHER LEARNING
HIGHER YEARNING

Bathroom "out back"

Old Fred Bessler was out watering his lawn when the big Packard rolled to a stop in front of the Kamstra house. "Fat Fred", we Kamstra kids called him. He was always watering his damn lawn – one sprinkler can at a time – pulling weeds and fussing with shrubs. Nice enough old guy; lived alone since his wife died some years ago. At 14, I didn't waste my time analyzing people's life styles; for me, "life styles" hadn't been invented yet. If they had and if I were into that sorta' thing, I might have observed that Fred's manicured lawn was only the most visible difference between the life style of the Besslers and the Kamstras next door.

We weren't slobs or anything; it's just that we weren't fanatics about our lawn either. After the infamous auction brought an end to Mom and Dad's farming career some four years earlier, they managed to scrape up enough to buy a house in Canby; population 643, mostly dependent on trade from southwestern Minnesota farmers who populated Yellow Medicine County. It wasn't much of a house and it wasn't in the best part of town. But, then, for $700 total cost, what the hell. The house was as modest as the price; bedroom, living room and kitchen/dining room downstairs; upstairs a "watch-your-head" open space for two beds plus floor space for added Kamstras as needed. Bathroom? A "two-holer" biffy just a short sprint across the back yard. Running water hadn't come to this part of town, but just about every home had its well and hand pump.

Dad managed to spare some of our household belongings from the auction block; bank debts be damned! His favorites were the trusty "parlor furnace" and the wood-burning kitchen stove. Dad had a genius for stoking fires. His toasty warm early morning fires and his "full bodied" coffee had a way of making everything all right with the world; no matter what your day had in store for you. He probably would have scoffed at central heating had it ever been available to him. The ornate parlor furnace was installed in the living room where – in conjunction with the kitchen stove – it continued to warm assorted Kamstra bottoms early mornings and especially at bath time. I marveled at the way he could break a sizeable piece of wood over his knee as he force fed both fires. What heat made its way upstairs kept those quarters just above freezing on the coldest days.

Brother, Hank, would be a guest upstairs; but not to worry about the heat this balmy September day. Hank blasted the trumpet horns of his gleaming Packard touring sedan and bounded toward the house. He was 27 now; more mature than when he piloted the stripped down Model T but no less in love with cars. The proud Packard stood as evidence that Hank's AED affliction was still a strong influence in his life. I had the disease, too, but no money to administer to its cravings. I wondered if Hank missed the Model T "sports car" the way I did. Funny how the Auto Erotic Gene skipped over most of the seven Kamstra boys. Most were content with ordinary "transportation" vehicles. Leslie, 20, cared little about cars except as a means of getting around and, of course, getting girls. He was obsessed with his goal of becoming the first Kamstra with a college degree. It was a goal he would ultimately reach and exceed; first to a doctorate and then a full professorship.

It seemed to me, he had been going to school forever. He funded his educational obsession with any job available from gutting chickens to digging ditches. And he made his meager pay stretch via living quarters not really intended for human habitation combined with meager food rations. These were the days before the Nanny Nation with its government sponsored student loans and subsidies for the poor.

Les would be joining Hank in helping me to launch my "higher education" into high school. He never missed an opportunity to urge me to join him in his educational quest. I knew he was right, but education to me was largely a pain in the ass that stood in the way of my seeing the world. Longing over-ruled logic as I instead envied Hank's "worldly" exploits.

Hank was the adventurous one. Sometimes he would write from a ski lodge out west where he had conned his way as a "chef". Other times, he would be in California, trying his hand at salesmanship. The folks never knew what postmark his next letter would have. Often, he would include a picture of himself and his latest auto acquisition. America was emerging from its "Golden Age" of automotive evolution. People who were royal, famous or just plain rich wallowed in this era. Oftentimes, they ordered their luxury cars custom built to their own – sometimes peculiar – tastes. Hank, on the other hand, was a cash-starved vagabond and a dreamer; always inventing things,

Hank blasted the trumpet horns of his gleaming Packard

scheming to make it big. His cars – impressive though never new – were none-the-less statements of his aspirations. And, of course, his affliction.

The massive, magnificent Packard was his latest statement. What a statement! Hank knew how to make this old Packard hum. He had fussed with and fixed every evidence of sloth and indifference left over from the former owner. Probably some guy who just got bored with it; maybe wanted the newest Packard or Cord or Duesenberg. Since Packard came on the scene in 1900, there had been more than 500 other marques launched. Most, of course, died shortly after birth.

Hank knew how to make his Packard purr but there is no way he could have been fully aware of its history and pedigree. When "Hank's Packard" came off the assembly line in 1930, Packard was the absolute prestige car leader of the world. Royal families worldwide owned them; used them for everything from state affairs to tiger hunts. American presidents revered the Packard, too; old Franklin D. Roosevelt was said to keep ten of them in the While House garage. Babe Ruth owned one; so did Gene Autry, Clark Gable, Errol Flynn, Jean Harlow. Even Joseph Stalin was a Packard guy.

History does not record whether any of these great or near great owners were actually carrying the Auto Erotic Gene. Probably damn few. Status was the thing.

Hank's Packard made its debut – with trumpet horns blaring from behind the commanding grill – on September 12, 1940. The Packard was officially designated as an Eight Series Model 826 Sedan; a 1930 model although Packard only identified "Series" in those days. The 826 was not one of Packard's most luxurious models, but its elegance overpowered me as well as the shabby street where we lived.

"Hank is here!" I wanted to run up to old Fred and say, "stop gawking, Fat Fred, haven't you ever seen a Packard limousine before?"

"Haven't you ever seen a Packard limousine before?"

I would catch Fred peeking out his kitchen window on days when Mom came home wheeling our coaster wagon full of "surplus" dried beans, lard and other welfare goodies. Fred, an economically "comfortable "retired farmer, had an almost new, seldom used Model A Ford in his garage. I wanted him to know we Kamstras had wheels too. Isolated on our farm, I had scarcely been aware of our threadbare financial state, except maybe comparing lunches at the one-room country school.

But this was a milestone day. No time to think about rich or poor. I was about to enroll in high school; what's more a high school in a different town. Adventure! The town was Okabena, an even smaller Minnesota town than Canby. Why Okabena? Tradition, Hank and Les explained. Both had worked their way through high school, living in the school janitor's home and earning their keep as assistant janitors. A worthy tradition and one that eased the burden on Mom and Dad who had miraculously fed and housed and loved eleven Kamstra children. With my departure, only 12-year-old kid sister, Phyllis, remained at home full time. All others had found jobs and/or mates that launched them on their own.

The Packard took up all the curb space allotted to the Kamstra abode

Darlene was there!

While Hank was catching up on the home town news in the kitchen, I snatched up the box containing my meager school wardrobe and headed out to the majestic Packard. From its authoritative grill, back along the side-mounted tire to the sloping rear fenders and gleaming rear bumpers, the Packard took up all the curb space allotted to the narrow Kamstra abode. I mounted the driver's side running board and reverently opened the door.

"Cars," I thought, "what a wonderful invention for mankind!" This was the carriage that was about to take me to a new adventure in my life. Getting there would be more than half the fun.

I slid my skinny butt into the driver's throne-like seat. Heaven on earth! Adrenaline from the excitement of it all counteracted my lack of sleep brought about by the previous night's anticipation. I grasped the oversized steering wheel and sighted down the long, commanding hood. The graceful Cormorant hood ornament – Hank said it had been silver plated – caught the sun just right; so did the metallic burgundy paint that Hank had polished to mirror perfection. Next, my attention – hell, my very soul – was gripped by the interior mystique of this magnificent machine. The smell of it. Leather. Refined, top grain, pamper-your-fanny leather; not the coarse, sweat-soaked harness leather that hung in our barn. This was class. This was a machine for exploring the world.

What must it have been like to just walk in and buy this car? Order it brand new. Specify the color, the chrome side mirrors. every convenience for touring America. Everywhere on the dashboard were handsome, chrome-trimmed gauges; gauges to tell the master of this machine the pressure of his oil, the temperature of the cooling water, the electrical amps…and, of course, his cruising speed. The speedometer read 100 miles per hour. Knowing Hank, he had probably determined whether the big, straight eight could hit 100 or not.

I turned my attention to the passenger seat.

Darlene was there!

Darlene Hoffermeir from the eighth grade. Darlene who needed a bra long before the other girls in her class. Darlene who, coming or going, did wonders

The "poverty pink" pact

for the pink flowered dress her mother made for her just before graduation. I knew that her mother made it and she knew that I knew. Welfare Moms all got bolts of that flowered "poverty pink" fabric. Not into fashion myself, it was still easy to see why this fabric found its way to the government surplus warehouses. It was more difficult to understand what kind of sadist would actually force this fabric on the economically deprived families of America. I wondered if old Franklin D. Roosevelt knew his "New Deal" had come to this.

Still, if anyone could make this cloth come alive, Darlene could. I will never forget that day she wore it.

"Were you embarrassed?" Darlene asked as her soft, slender fingers reached for mine.

"No, not at all," I lied.

She was referring to the fact that on the very same day she wore her flowered pink dress, I wore my flowered pink shirt made by my Mom.

Now her hand was gently touching mine.

"I don't think I can ever wear pink again," Darlene said. Darlene. Darlene Hoffermeir was confiding in me; me, Ken Kamstra, to whom she had never previously spoken a word in her life. We were cementing a kinship; a poverty pact as it were.

"Me neither," I replied, instantly realizing the stupidity of my words. Dumb shit! Dunderhead! Why couldn't I say something more profound; something worthy of this milestone pact with Darlene. Couldn't you have at least told her how lovely she looked in that dress. "Me neither". Is it any damn wonder you've never had a girl friend?

Nonetheless, I slipped Darlene's hand further into mine. What happened next was almost too delightful to retell. As our fingers entwined, they seemed to take on a lascivious life of their own, intent on mutual exploration and response.

Darlene had vanished… Okabena here we come

I had never actually touched a girl before; fantasized, but never actually touched one. While our fingers continued their shameless wrestling, some primal instinct compelled me to pull Darlene closer to me. I became aware for the first time how her breathing created a rhythmic, mesmerizing rise and fall of her bosom. Our faces were now only inches apart. Her deep blue eyes seemed to be saying "go ahead, kiss me."

"Hey, Kenny, snap out of it! Time to get on the road."

Hank's words cruelly pierced my fantasy and Darlene was gone. I mumbled something about "dozing off" and scrambled over into the passenger's seat. Damn! Just when Darlene was going to kiss me. Now I would never know the ecstasy of it. I was going to Okabena High; Darlene would continue on at Canby. Why couldn't Hank have waited just a few minutes more? The day we both wore "poverty pink" was real. Today was fantasy and I would probably never see Darlene again.

So Darlene had vanished. So what, I tried to convince myself. Girls didn't know anything about cars or care anything about cars anyway.

"Okabena, here we come, Kenny," Hank said, slapping my knee. It was an obvious effort to snap me out of my funk.

"Okabena", what a dumb name for a school, I thought. I didn't like the name "Kenny" either. I never told Hank or anyone how I hated the name "Kenny", and now didn't seem the time. Mom told me I was "sickly" at birth; I knew only that I was skinny and maybe even a bit of a sissy. "Kenny" – pronounced with a demeaning, "haw haw" sneer – always preceded a pummeling by the school bully. Every school, it seemed, had this ruthless ritual of putting "the new kid" in his place. And I always seemed to be the new kid as my family moved from place to place trying to make a go of depression era farming.

Here I was about to be the "new kid" at Okabena High School. My mail order Charles Atlas Body Building Course added a muscle or two, but I was still no real threat to any determined bully.

A time before Auto Immune barbarians

We were out of town now; headed due south. Hank's foot went to the floorboard and the needle on the big Packard speedometer climbed to 85. The cavernous inside maintained a dignified near silence. Combined with the thrill of the ride was the satisfaction of being the center of attention from my two brothers. I was off to another town to start high school. Adventure! Best of all, the adventure would be delivered in a spit and polish Packard, the likes of which I had never before even imagined.

Decades from this day, Packards would be collected as classics. I was enjoying the experience in "real time". Old Packards in 1940 were just old Packards. No one could know that Packard, along with most of the Golden Era classic car companies, would cease to exist.

These were happy, uncomplicated times. None of us could have foreseen that Auto Immune Barbarians would one day push for legislation to outlaw and confiscate old cars. Who – even in their worst nightmare – could imagine fellow humans crushing and "cubing" cars like this. All in the name of environmental protection. As this is written, the "Left Coast" California sponsors are still trying to get these "old polluters" off the road. The "Kewbash" Cargoyle is waiting and watching.

We Kamstras never spent much time thinking or talking politics. Our protracted and intimate familiarity with scarce funds undoubtedly categorized us as Democrats. Dad, for one, believed that Franklin Delano Roosevelt was next to – and maybe even a step ahead of – God. To his way of thinking, "rich" and "S.O.B" were synonymous. As we cruised along in our pretentious carriage, I wasn't sure whether I wanted to hate the rich or somehow try to join them.

Cars were surely dream machines. Whatever life had in store for me, somehow I knew cars would help get me there. Or at least they would make the journey so much sweeter.

■ ■ ■

Kewbash

Kewbash loves his work. Over the sounds of crunching metal and breaking glass, he hums and cackles all day long. His job is crushing old cars into to neat little cubes. Government job. Recycling and all that. This Cargoyle was hatched in California; drew its first gurgling breath on the infamous "Left Coast"; where else? The new law would ordain the confiscation – and cubing – of old cars; all in the name of planet-saving. Inhabitants of this sun-kissed land of auto affectionados and car collectors are nervous. Eco-freaks are delirious. They fantasize about how serene life will be once they are rid of all those old cars and those horrible people who are always parading around in them.

■ ■ ■

Your car is old, quite clearly dated. Beware lest it be confiscated.

The law proposed, it leaves no doubt. They'll crush it, cube it, throw it out.

CHAPTER 5

BATHROOMS, THE PLACE FOR SOME OF YOUR BEST THINKING

"Time to see what the rest of the world is all about"

It happened in the girls' bathroom at Okabena High. That's when I decided, no more of this.

"Two years of high school is enough for me. Time to see what the rest of the world is all about."

That momentous, life-altering decision came about as I was extracting a sanitary napkin, the root cause of a plugged toilet and general flooding conditions in the girls biffy. All in a day's after school work for Ken Kamstra, assistant janitor. I wanted to call Hank and say, "come and get me. and, oh by the way, bring the Packard".

"Girls are such damn slobs!", I grumbled. "High school guys think girls are all so pretty, prissy and pink. They should damn well have to clean up after them."

Of course, the guys would never know except maybe after they get married and then it would be too late. Well, you wouldn't catch me marrying one of them any time soon. In the boys' locker room – where I changed for football practice – guys would guffaw about what a titillating trip it would be to somehow hide out in the girls' can. Little did they know.

Author's note: My reference to football was not a contrived excuse to bring up my heroic days as Okabena's championship-winning quarterback. My brief football career was spent mostly on the bench. Okabena was so tiny, they played in the nine-man league. Farm kids on most teams were big, mean and out to hurt somebody if they could. When they succeeded, I was the substitute, "cannon fodder" lineman sent in to take the beatings until the regular lineman recovered.

Back to the girl's bathroom. These rooms held no prurient fascination for me. Cleaning and scrubbing bathrooms, boys and girls, was part of my job of course. The Kamstra Son's tradition and all that. A shitty job nonetheless. I was up at the crack of dawn, earlier if there had been heavy snow. No sissy snow blowers at Okabena High; we shoveled every ton of it by hand. Then there were furnaces to stoke in the morning and ashes to haul out after school. Shovel, stoke, sweep, scrub; it was what you did if you were a "Kamstra Kid" earning his room and board. I didn't resent it; but two year's worth was about enough for this "Kamstra Kid."

One Sunday morning – December 7, 1941 – George Stevenson, my wiry, hyper energetic janitor boss, was listening to the early morning news when I burst in to babble about something.

"Shut up!", George said and as he turned I saw the color had drained from his face. George had cussed me out for some goof or infraction now and then. He and his wife, Lydia, were kind and caring folks. They fed me well. Never before had I been told to "shut up". This must be serious news, I thought; I never really paid much attention to news. It didn't seem to have any relevance to my life.

"This day will live in infamy!"

President Roosevelt was addressing the nation. I wasn't sure exactly what "infamy" meant, but I joined the Stevensons in silent, somber attention.

"The Japs are bombing our ships in Pearl Harbor", George said. Lydia stood by his chair, hand on George's shoulder. There were tears in her eyes. America was now at war. War dominated the news every day after that. Still the Okabena High routine went on much as before. Same horse play in the hallways, same homework, same grunge work. Guys coming up on 18 started to sweat the draft. Some rushed off to enlist. None of us knew it, of course, but millions would be maimed or killed before it was all over.

In June, my sophomore year had ended and I headed back to Canby and home. All I knew for sure is that I wasn't coming back to Okabena. I missed my family and our "togetherness" days on our old farm. I missed our hot rod Model T and the "free range" living it symbolized. I even missed the cantankerous Fordson tractor. There wasn't much Kamstra presence left in Canby. Most of my brothers had "gone to war" as the Canby News liked to phrase it.

Les, now with a B-29 Bomber squadron, shared some of his meager GI pay with me; sending an occasional "fiver" along with predictable advice for me to stay in high school and try to make something of myself. Helping the younger brother financially was also part of the Kamstras-in-Okabena tradition.

"This day will live in infamy!"

My ticket to "automobility"

I took the five but ignored the advice. My AED addiction was demanding treatment. I needed to get to the money-earning, car-buying stage of my life. The war, of course, made this kind of mindless teenage yearning far easier to fulfill. All available adult manpower was being drafted – or in some cases volunteering – into the armed services.

I found an ad offering work in Seattle's shipyards building warships. This, I said, may be my ticket to "automobility" and some much needed attention to my AED disease. All I needed was a way to get to Seattle.

Herman Foose was born about 30 years ahead of his time. He should have been sealed in a time capsule and re-introduced to society in the mid seventies. Ugly as he was, he could have been the liberals' poster boy when in 1974 they ordained that no driver should ever again exceed 55 miles per hour. Herman was decades ahead of them. He adopted the 55 mile limit as his own in 1943. Without question, he was an Auto Immune.

His weenie approach to driving might have been of no concern to me except for one sad, salient fact. He was my "designated driver" from Minnesota to Seattle.

I was at last escaping the classroom – and in my case, bathroom – drudgery of high school. What Herman was escaping from I never learned. He didn't talk much. It was World War II war time and just about everyone's normal life routines were disrupted. Time for me to slip away. America's production capacity – including car manufacture – had been commandeered for making tanks, guns, planes and ships. Cars were becoming scarce.

Enterprising Midwest car dealers seized upon the opportunity to sell their used cars where the defense plant workers – and the bigger bucks – were. That's where Herman and I came in. Dealers in Minnesota ran ads offering free transportation to anyone willing to drive theirs cars to West Coast "war plant" cities. Herman, who worked for a box making company somewhere in Minneapolis, was immediately accepted by the dealer as a mature and responsible guy. Someone who could get a car safely to the Seattle with no shenanigans, side trips or recklessness. The skinny kid behind him in line – me – was another matter.

"We can't have no 16-year-olds driving our best cars across country," the dealer said; his voice left little doubt that there was any room for negotiation.

My escape plan – the master plan to earn money for my own wheels – seemed to be dissolving before it even began. In desperation, I pleaded with "Big Ted", the dealer, who finally relented allowing as how I could keep Herman company, but only as a passenger.

"And, Herman, don't ever let me hear that you let this young punk behind the wheel. You hear?" This may have been the day that my contempt for used car dealers was born.

"And you're paying your own way, kid. This ain't no sweetheart vacation deal. There's little enough money in selling cars as it is."

Big Ted, had nothing to worry about. Herman, it turned out, was a man who lived by the rules. Herman was a puffy, pudgy person. With a wig, he could easily have passed for someone's maiden aunt; maybe fussing over a batch of brownies just out of the oven. His pudgy fingers gripped the steering wheel of our 1939 "cream puff" Chevrolet like grim death. Death, however, seemed a very remote threat with Herman at the wheel. We headed west out of Minneapolis.

The day that my contempt for used car dealers was born

"Maybe Herman is just nervous driving in big cities as I would be. Pretty soon, when we hit the open spaces, he'll tromp on the gas and we'll get rolling." I was trying to convince myself.

Wrong! This was as fast as Herman ever drove; probably in his whole life. He was not about to take any chances on losing

A Painter Creates "Yesteryear" Nostalgia; Memories And Fantasies That Live On In The Hearts Of Car Lovers Everywhere

"Regular Meals"

Ever long for quiet country roads that "used to be"? Roads that at every turn unveil long abandoned gas stations, eateries, farm buildings. And snuggled next to each of them rusting cars from the 30's, 40's and 50's. "Junk" to the Auto Immune; treasures to the glazed over eyes of the Auto Erotic.

Dale Klee recreates these serene scenes from his studio in Wyoming, Minnesota. Paintings and prints that often sell out in a matter of months. It all began for the 55-year-old Klee working in his dad's rural Michigan gas station. So young, he could scarcely reach high enough to clean the windshields of customer cars, he nonetheless developed a passion for cars. Especially cars of the 30's.

To please dad, he majored in business administration in college. To please himself, he turned to painting. Painting old cars. Today it's his business, his profession, his life.

"As we grow older, the things of our youth become more precious. We like to return to them in our memories," said Dale.

Klee makes those memories more vivid; enjoyable to car lovers of any age.

Artist Dale Klee.

"The Red Barn"

control of Big Ted's Chevy; a Chevy whose previous little-old-lady owner "drove it only to church on Sundays". We were off to Seattle and we would get there at Herman's pace and not one minute sooner.

"This must have been what it was like when the pioneers headed west in their covered wagons," I thought. "Only a might faster."

I guessed Herman to be pushing 50; no immediate worries about the draft for now. He stood maybe 5' 10" but looked even shorter as he hunched over the steering wheel. He was balding and bulging at the chin and belly. I wondered if eating was his only vice; hoping that if he did have another vice it wasn't a hankering for teen-aged boys.

If Herman had a wife or kids or family, he didn't mention it and I didn't ask. Not surprisingly, he was part of the West Coast defense plant migration. At least we had something in common. I didn't know what he would do with the money he hoped to make; I knew what I would buy.

Two thousand miles at 55 miles per hour gives one time to think. I thought "I don't want to grow old and boring like Herman." Whatever life has in store for me – however I carve out my own destiny – I want it to be out of the ordinary. It should involve interesting people…and lots and lots of interesting cars.

■ ■ ■

Two thousand miles at 55 miles per hour

CHAPTER 6

Hard Hat Lessons On The Realities Of Life

My AED psyche was screaming for a car

The lumbering city bus, one of dozens, disgorged me and hundred of others at the gates of the sprawling ship-building operation. July 11, 1942, Seattle, Washington. A 16-year-old Minnesota hick, I tried to swagger my walk as I headed for the employee gate. I stepped away from the pushing throng, lit a cigarette with as much macho and nonchalance as I could muster; tried not to cough since I was just learning. I was in awe. Overwhelmed by my surroundings.

It was eerie. The rain and the darkness were unrelenting. Intermittent yellow/green light bursts from hundreds of arc welders only accentuated the bleak, black night. Hard hat workers slogged through the ever present puddles and ponds; their destination one of the scores of warships – destroyers and tenders – under construction.

Did I really want to go through with this just to have a car of my own? Swagger and dangling cigarette notwithstanding, I was already homesick. And scared. My AED-dominated psyche was screaming for a car. Dad thought cars were damn foolishness. Canby folks, after all, could walk the length and breadth of the town in well under an hour.

Standing in the Seattle rain – it rains all the time in Seattle – I tried to bring my car vision back into focus. It had been very clear when I sat in the abandoned junkers at "Canby Auto Salvage." Now the focus was blurred. Maybe it was the rain.

Air raid defense balloons, suspended everywhere over the city, provided an ominous finishing touch to this other-worldly scene. America was now officially at war; a war declared only hours after Japan's sneak attack on Hawaii's Pearl Harbor Navy Base on December 7, 1941.

We were a country unprepared. We were a country struggling to catch up. Ships, planes, trucks, tanks, guns, ammunition, equipment, uniforms. The list of wartime needs was endless; the work schedule to produce these materials was 24 hours a day, seven days a week. Before it was too late. Just about anyone not in uniform could find work. Women worked side by side with men. This was the most massive war production effort in history.

It was 10:45 PM. The "graveyard" shift – 11: p.m. to 7 a.m. – was streaming through the shipyard gates, punching in their time cards and reporting for work. Workers painted their names on their hard hats. There was a general camaraderie as everyone headed for his or her assigned task. No one needed to be told why their work was important. If we lost this war, we lost our freedom forever. We would be – those who survived the battles and the slave labor camps – citizens under Hitler's "Master Race" scheme.

In the midst of this historic setting, Ken Kamstra slogged upon the scene. In all honesty, I was more interested in making money than making war or making history. I had a life to get started; a dream to fulfill. First order of business: make enough money to buy a car. Standing 6 feet tall and tipping the scales at 137, I was about to experience the real life of "blue color" industrial labor. I already knew about labor: farm labor, garbage truck labor, coal-car-unloading labor and more. These were the kinds of "odd jobs" my dad picked up in Canby after the demise of the Kamstra farming venture. I worked side by side with Dad. Whatever pay he got went directly into the family survival fund; nothing left over for the struggling helper. In spite of all this "labor" experience, I didn't know about regimented, punch card, unionized labor.

I would learn.

My boss, a lanky old Southerner with a perpetual scowl, led me up the makeshift gang plank and then down steel ladders into the bowels of the ship. Heavy boots not withstanding, I tried not to trip or stumble. No sense feeding Frank's contempt. As we made our way across the tangled cables and clutter on the ship's deck, he looked at me with a scorn born of supervising too many "defense workers". Old men, women and young punks like me. A work force that didn't know a damn thing about building warships or any other kind of ships for that matter. Our conversation thus far was confined to a cryptic introduction.

"Ma name's Frank. Ah'm chief electrician and ah'm your boss. That's all you got to know!" He fumbled with my work papers. "Sez hyere that you all are from Minnesota. Probably never seen a gol damn ship before! Right? Your name's Kenny, right?"

"Your name's Kenny, right?"

Bravado but still only 16

That damned name, "Kenny", again! I wouldn't challenge Frank on it just now. Concentrate; try not to catch your big boots in a cable or miss a rung on the ladder.

We stopped near a husky young man. His wrestling match with a bundle of steel-encased electrical cables commanded his full attention. Looking at his back, I could see he was muscular and had an oversized mop of brown curly hair.

"Andy!" Frank's voice reverberated off the ship's bulkheads (you learned not to call them "walls") and it rose above the constant din of rivet guns, hammers, welders and what not. Frank now had Andy's full attention. "Andy, this hyere's Kenny your new helper. See he earns his pay."

Andy's grin was like a welcome ray of sunshine. As soon as Frank's massive work boots disappeared up the ladder, Andy shook my hand, smiled even broader and spoke.

"Name's Andrew, Andrew Freelson. Everybody calls me Andy. Don't let old Frank get to you. He comes off like a mean sonofabitch but he's a good boss if you do your work."

I stood there with my heavy coveralls, clumsy boots and a shit-eating grin on my face. I was one lonely, homesick kid who needed a friend like nobody else in the world right now. In spite of all my bravado, making my way in the cruel world all by myself, I was still a 16-year-old kid who had never been this far from home before. Never saw a ship – Frank was right – never saw a body of water as big as Seattle's Puget Sound, much less the Pacific Ocean just beyond. Never saw much of anything except farms and the streets of tiny Canby, Minnesota. But I did have this car dream.

"Call me, Ken." I said, hoping he would never call me "Kenny" and never guess how much I was aching to become his friend.

We did become good friends. Andy was my mentor, too. Not long after I came to work at the shipyards, he helped me approach the union bosses and apply for a journeyman's rating.

"All you have to do is agree to pay more dues and you're in," said Andy.

He was right. In a few days, I was certified as a journeyman marine electrician; making more money than I ever dreamed I could make.

"This is a joke, right? A goddamn, cotton-pickin' joke! What in hell can you do aboard this ship that makes you a goddamn journeyman? Christ sakes!"

Frank was mad as hell and he was right. My journeyman rating was a joke. Still, if the union was willing to make me a journeyman for a few extra bucks out of my paycheck, who was I to argue?

I was learning the rules of hard hat living.

"Shit. He'll get used to it," Andy said, proud of the progress of his student and friend. We both had a good laugh.

Truth be known, we were both "grunt workers" and nowhere near electricians at any level. We pulled massive electrical cables on board, tugged and bent them into their assigned positions. Sometimes, we spent a whole shift wrapping open wire cable ends, readying them for connection to the ship's massive control boards. Thus did we make our modest contribution to the war effort.

Learning the rules of hard hat living

■ ■ ■

The mood of the country was patriotism, patriotism, patriotism. It reached into middle class neighborhoods where folks were willing to surrender their privacy. Family bedrooms were rented to defense workers; family kitchens and dining rooms were shared under room-and-board arrangements. These were not hard nosed, experienced landlords; just nice families trying to do their part. Such a family was the Taalkinan family, Sara and Hjalmer and their only child, Peggy, 16. I answered their ad and found a home in one of their upstairs bedrooms. They treated me well, fed me well and even packed my lunch for the graveyard shift.

What To Do When Your Cars Multiply;
The Ellingson Method.

Every car buff – including the author – has a "garage too small" problem. America, in fact, is dotted with thousands of pole barns housing personal car collections. Many of these collections are nondescript, having more sentimental value than cash value.

Then there is the Ellingson collection. Eugene Ellingson, 66, a lifetime mechanic and probable AED addict, started his collection in a pole barn too. Then somewhere around 30 cars, he decided they needed a better home. Really better. So he built the Ellingson Car Museum in Rogers, Minnesota. Its glass-walled showroom faces an Interstate heading north from Minneapolis. Inside, nearly all the Ellingson cars – with both sentimental and big buck value – can be displayed at once. Imaginatively displayed. Costumed mannequins add to the ever-changing settings. Consignment vehicles bring the rotating display to more than 100 cars. Over 300 vehicles have been displayed since the museum's opening in 1995. Million dollar Mercedes classics share space with Model T Ford trucks, sixties "muscle cars", motorcycles and more.

Much more. There's an authentic – and working – soda fountain, a souvenir/gift shop, a book store. Enthusiasts can come and reminisce or even buy a car. Son, Scott, operates the museum. His wife, Diana, has a bridal shop that just happens to include availability of classic cars for the wedding party.

Down the hall from my room, another "defense worker" – called himself Ed Kransberg – rented a room. He looked "draft age", but seemed to have found a way to avoid it. Ed – he was pale even by sun-deprived Seattle standards – wasn't the social type. Except for meals and going to work, Ed rarely emerged from his room. I made some overtures. Once, even confided in him my cherished dreams of buying a car of my own. No response.

Who needed Ed? I was socking away money to make a dream come true.

Even in the car-starved 1940's, a guy could buy himself a damn nice used car for the nearly $300 I had saved. It was starting to happen: my dream of owning my own wheels. Fast wheels! The memory of my roaring, wild rides aboard brother Hank's stripped down Model-T was still very much alive.

Hank was now with General Patton's army. I was proud when he made officer candidate school and got his lieutenant's bars; prouder still when he received a battlefield promotion to captain. If he were still home, he would be the first person to see my "new" car when I bought it.

My dream of owning my own wheels... fast wheels!

From pole barn to posh museum, Eugene Ellingson, left, displays his and others' cars in splendor. There's even a "yesteryear" soda fountain for hungry/ thirsty visitors.

Dreams energize your life

Any day now, I could tell old Frank to take his job – journeyman wages and all – and shove it. Ken Kamstra – not "Kenny" – was in a hurry to get on with life. The jobs I had experienced so far in my life were downright boring. Boring as hell! How, I asked myself, could people spend years, decades, maybe even an entire lifetime, doing boring, repetitive work.

I knew the answer. People did it because they needed money, money that best came from regular paychecks. Most had families to feed, mortgages to pay off. Their circumstances doomed them to a perpetual – and agonizingly uneventful – life of paycheck dependence.

I wanted no part of this treadmill. At 16, I hadn't come to many hard conclusions about life, but this was one of them. Maybe there really was a hereafter, but that was no excuse to fritter away the here and now.

Owning a car was not a lofty dream, to be sure. Still, it would accelerate life's adventure, especially if one were heavy on the gas pedal. Each morning after work, I would recount my stash just for reassurance. Each bill was counted, tucked back in my "budget book" and hidden in a bureau drawer. Stealth. Pure stealth. Pure joy.

I wondered if pale, shifty-eyed Ed ever had a dream. Dreams energize your life. They're exciting. With this profound thought, I drifted off to sleep. Had to catch a few winks before it was graveyard shift time again. Before I knew it, I was on the bus heading for the shipyards. Somehow this time it was different, though. I didn't really have to work this job anymore. It was my call when I would hang it up and head back to Canby.

Morning. Graveyard shift over. The bus, spewing it's stinky black diesel smoke, delivered me back to my board-and-room life; a life that had become quite comfortable to me now. Of course, everything about life is cozy and comfortable when you have money stashed away.

It was Wednesday, one of my favorite breakfast days of the week. Mrs. Taalkinan was a good cook but on Wednesday's she made pancakes and sausages that were pure heaven. We sat at the kitchen table, Mrs. Taalkinan, her daughter, Peggy, and always-hungry Ken Kamstra.

Panic and pancakes at the Taalkinan table

Ed wasn't at the table. There was a tension so heavy in the air, it almost took the fun out of the pancakes. Mrs. Taalkinan spoke first. She was angry and upset.

"Ed skipped out last night." she solemnly announced. "Owed me almost three week's rent. Kept asking for extensions on his rent and I kept giving in. Damn him! Damn him!" That was as close as Mrs. Taalkinan ever came to profanity or speaking ill of another human. Sara and Hjalmer were religious people. They didn't swear. They didn't drink. They trusted their fellow man. But they watched their money and three week's rent was a big loss.

"I'm sorry," I said lamely, my mouth full of pancakes. "He wasn't a very friendly cuss; maybe the next roomer will be more fun."

My consolation went over like the proverbial lead balloon. Peggy said nothing but you could tell they were both shaken. They had turned their home into a rooming house to help the war effort, otherwise they wouldn't have given up their privacy for any price. Now, they had to wonder. As I headed upstairs to my room, I hoped I would not be painted with Ed's brush. Surely, they knew I would never skip out on them or do anything dishonest.

I did, however, cast an occasional boy-girl glance at daughter, Peggy. At 16, she was attracting some attention from boys according to family dinner table talk. It was all beside the point in any event; Peggy had decided that Andy was the guy for her. Not only was he better looking and better built than me, he had his own – albeit well used – Plymouth sport coupe complete with rumble seat. I envied Andy more for his car than his hand-holding with Peggy. Girls caught my attention from time to time but I wasn't as yet obsessed with them.

Peggy was even more beside the point because this was one roomer who had made his bundle and was about to head for home. I would, of course, do it with proper notice to my landlady. Would my departure bring an end to the Taalkinan rooming house business? I wondered.

Anyway, I was tired; decided to get my daytime sack time in early.

> **Let those beautiful bills flutter down onto my bed**

Mid afternoon, I awoke and at once the excitement of buying my first car and returning home "the conquering hero" swept over me. I reached for the bureau drawer handle; time for the counting ritual. It never changed. Open the book, let those beautiful bills flutter down onto my bed. The joy it brought me was enhanced a thousand fold by childhood experience. This was a kid who had rarely seen one ten dollar bill much less – by latest ecstatic count – 29 of them. I held the book even higher than usual just to savor the pure pleasure of watching the bills flow out. Book up, pages flipped open.

No bills came out! Not even one!

Panic swept over me. I rushed to the bureau and began throwing out my clothes like a mad man. Logic told me that all these bills could not have miraculously escaped from the book and hidden themselves among my clothes. I wasn't using logic; I was crazy with shock. I flipped open each page one by one; tore some out in an act of pure rage.

"My money's gone!" I almost screamed.

Strangely, my near hysteria was mixed with embarrassment. What would the Taalkinans think about a guy dumb enough to hide his money with his socks and underwear? I was stumbling down the stairs near tears. To hell with grown up stoicism. To hell with manly pride. Right now, I was just a 16-year-old kid who had been ripped off. Half way down the stairs, it finally dawned on me.

"It was Ed! That sonofabich Ed! "

I said nothing to anyone. Over time, I faced up to the facts. I would never see my money again. The Seattle police had more important work than tracking down sneaky Ed. Irony of ironies they did send out a juvenile officer to confront the Taalkinans about the under age juvenile they were harboring in their upstairs bedroom.

"City law says he must be in school, Mrs. Taalkinan."

That's all my landlady needed after being ripped off by her other boarder. I filled out the papers and dutifully showed up in the early afternoon class. After two sessions, I never showed up again and I never heard from the juvenile authorities again. They had fulfilled their obligations; I had fulfilled mine.

Never a day went by that I didn't wish for some unspeakable, horrible fate to befall Ed. All the while, I knew the bastard was probably having one helluva' good time partying with my money. How would a zombie like Ed party anyway?

I was at least learning some of the more unpleasant lessons of life. Lesson one: the world population has in its midst a disproportionate number of thieves and downright assholes. Lesson two: when life shafts you, get over it. Get on with it. And be damn careful who you trust.

I couldn't have been convinced of it at the time, but the life lesson Ed taught me was probably worth $290. I would be a "somebody" someday. I didn't know who or just how I would accomplish it. I only knew I would not get there depending on regular paychecks…or rooming with the likes of Ed. Ed taught me all I would ever need to know about the asshole perspective.

I did the graveyard shift for another stint; scrimping and saving even more every week. This time, it went into a neighborhood bank. Finally, in late May – I was 17 now – I had amassed another stash.

Older, one hell of a lot wiser and somewhat poorer than planned, I was heading for the long awaited, triumphant return to Canby.

When life shafts you, get over it

CHAPTER 7

WHERE HAVE ALL THE MENFOLK GONE?

I had the V-8 – my very own '34 Ford V-8 – throttled down. A sweet, melodious rumble burbled from the exhaust as I cruised through Canby's "business district"; all two blocks of it. The street never looked more magnificent. From the theater marquee, cascading lights called attention to a Gene Autry double feature. Red Owl Foods still anchored the end of the block, just down from Hall's Drugs and Larry's Pool, Bar & Eats. The drug store served double duty as the Greyhound Bus Depot; the point from which my great Seattle adventure had begun.

■ ■ ■

A sweet, melodious rumble burbled from the exhausts

In Granite Falls, Minnesota, some 40 miles northeast of Canby, I prematurely ended my long bus journey from Seattle. The grand moment was at hand. Time to select my first car. An event of magnitude far greater than a first date or even first sex. The car had to be an appropriate vehicle for my triumphant return. One cannot, after all, be a conquering hero climbing off a bus.

"Busses are for people who aren't going anywhere", I bragged to myself as I walked from one used car lot to another. Most cars on the lots were dogs. Tired old family-four-doors that would do absolutely nothing to enhance the return of this native to his homeland. Teenager, to be sure, but one who had seen a few thousand miles of America; an adventurous maverick. It was essential that I have a car in keeping with my self image.

Anticipating the thrill of buying my first car was an emotion almost beyond my ability to contain it. My AED affliction only intensified the rush of adrenaline. I walked faster; almost running by the time I spotted it. The Robin's egg blue Ford with its slanted grill and sporty shape beckoned me. Come closer. Sit behind the wheel and sight down that lovely hood to the sleek chrome greyhound hood ornament. Before long, a salesman spotted me, sizing me up as he approached. He didn't buy my feigned indifference. I was almost drooling as I sat in the command position with my hand draped over the floor-mounted shift. I had to have this car. A perfunctory drive around the block, a look under the hood and we were in the salesman's cluttered office closing the deal on the car of my dreams. I paid cash, pretending there was lots more where that came from. There wasn't. Damn little left for gas or for my soon-to-be-auto-intensive life style. My thieving Seattle roommate had seen to that.

I brushed up – hell, I was really just learning – on my driving skills as the Ford and I made our way to Canby. Authorities weren't all that concerned about driver's licenses back then. I came into town via back roads. Just in case and just to maximize the fun. A tromp on the gas and the 85 horses roared to life with a high pitched whine. When the speedometer nudged into the 80's, I backed off. Save that for a bit more practice.

Something about the burble and rumble of a V8 stirs the hormones of red blooded car lovers. Since this wondrous Ford triggered my AED gene, I have indulged in all manner of auto-induced eroticism. My indulgence was so intense, I was unaware of doom squads conspiring to put an end to such wanton destruction of Mother Earth. Their battle cry: "Battery Power!" As the Twenty First Century dawns, cowering car makers are already marketing their battery-powered cars. Will new generations never know the thrill of a rumbling V8?

The car seemed to be running as well as the salesman said it would. Sometimes you luck out. Sometimes you get a lemon. Either way, the sales pitch is the same.

"Hey! Ken Kamstra's back in town!" I shouted to nobody. Nobody really gave a damn that I was back in town; or had ever left for that matter. Not surprising. The seven Kamstra brothers were always coming and going. Canby and the house where we lived was the nuclear center of all our lives. Lives we were too busy living to appreciate the core of strength represented by Mom and Dad.

We couldn't hit the folks up for a loan but we could expect an unconditional, unlimited welcome to their one-bedroom-plus-attic home. The welcome always included generous, no frills home cooking. Dad kept alive his farming skills by raising potatoes, tomatoes, squash, beets, beans, sweet corn and more. Our back yard and a few vacant lots around town were pressed into service for this life-sustaining mission. Odd jobs helped Dad fund the meat course when there was one.

"Well, Okay son, but be careful"

Assyd

Behold the ultimate weapon of Eco-Freaks everywhere: Assyd. Hatched in our nation's capitol, this Cargoyle's battery-powered brain is wired to put an end to your passion for cars. Forever. Assyd wants to yank you out of your beloved, gas-powered car. Not to worry; he'll put you into something more politically correct, something acid-powered. You won't move very far or very fast, but the ecology crowd will give you a thumbs up wherever you go. ■ "No thanks," you say, "I'd rather have a real car." ■ Assyd will only cackle at your naive rebuff. He knows you will soon have no choice. Assyd is not just the darling of the Auto-Immune, he's official government policy. Switch over to Assyd's "Goremobiles" has already begun…ready or not. Shouldn't you go out and hug your car right now?

■ ■ ■

It's cars not trees
that get your hugs.
So hang on tight
When Assyd tugs.

Electric cars
hold no appeal?
Well give a care
how Gore would feel.

Cruising my beautiful "Blue Bomber"

We couldn't borrow the family car of course. There wasn't one. Older family members found work and bought cars. Unaware of the relentless force of my AED affliction, I felt compelled to speed up the process of acquiring wheels. I didn't resent Dad's car-less poverty. It had always been so.

I did resent high school classmates – probably Auto Immunes at that – who had easy access to the family car.

"Hey, Dad. Got a heavy date tonight. Can I have the car? Please?"

"Well, okay, son, but be careful."

"You know, Martha, Delbert is a good boy. Maybe we should think about getting him a car of his own."

"Whatever you think, Hon."

I was cruising my beautiful "Blue Bomber" past Canby High. That's what rekindled my resentment of affluent parents and their snotty, spoiled kids; kids offered cars on a silver platter. It was, of course, irrational thinking. The same kind of thinking that cut my high school education in half and launched my Seattle expedition.

Rational thinking be damned, I was now cruising in my first car. A car I had earned the hard way. I savored every delicious minute of my triumphant return. Just six blocks north of the high school – nothing was very far away in a town the size of Canby – was home. As I pulled to a stop, a banner in our front window caught my eye. It had five stars on it. Five Kamstra sons in service. One son was already too old for service and I was still too young, almost.

Canby, like most towns in America, was being rapidly drained of all its military-eligible males. It did not escape my notice that a young stud like me – with his own car and all – could attract girls like never before. Summer rolled into fall and fall into winter. The beer-and-babes routine was all kinds of fun, but something was bugging me.

Maybe it was the five-star flag in the front window. Shouldn't I be star number six if I was a real man? Then, again, maybe it was just my way of rationalizing the lust for another big adventure.

The Canby I came back to wasn't the Canby I had left. Young fathers, some just starting married life, were being drafted as their numbers came up. Already, some of these recent brides had received the dreaded telegram that made them widows. Other guys were enlisting. Mom and Dad were proud of their patriotic window display. It wasn't often they could one-up their neighbors. This time they had the edge. They didn't like the idea of their youngest going off to war, but they were understanding.

Thus far in my life, I had contributed nothing of consequence to the citizens of Canby. Now, if I enlisted, I would at least let some poor devil off the draft hook for a few more weeks or months. I hoped it would be a deserving guy who just wanted a little more time with his wife and kids.

On December 7, 1943, the second anniversary of the Japanese attack on Pearl Harbor, I enlisted. Got my picture in the Minneapolis newspaper along with other young rubes who – in their desire to avenge the Japanese attack – were enlisting.

The Navy sent me home to clean up my affairs and enjoy a last Christmas at home before reporting back to Minneapolis on December 27. The "affair" I had to clean up was my Blue Bomber. There was no place to store it. Nor did I have any idea when I would be coming back. The Ford had to go. We enjoyed a short but beautiful life together and now it must end.

A local farmer answered my ad and bought the car within minutes of seeing it. I don't think he was impressed with the mirror finish or the racy lines. He just needed a car and good used cars were getting scarcer with each succeeding month of the war. The $100 profit I made on the sale helped to pay off the loan that had funded my few months of free wheeling living.

A few days later, it was off to the Navy.

■ ■ ■

The Ford had to go

CHAPTER 8

Learning Mechanics And Manhood The Hard Way

"Have you ever spent time in jail?"

It was New Year's Eve, 1943. Our troop train – stacks of bunks and damn few amenities – was rumbling and swaying across Montana on the way to the U.S Naval Training Station at Farrigut, Idaho. There, in the desolate hill country, we would get our boot camp training. Some guys had smuggled a bottle or two on board and were trying to make a party of it. Most, I suspected, were hiding their fear and apprehension with boisterousness.

Our comprehension of what was happening to us had not yet extended to the awful reality that some of us might not live to see another New Year's Eve.

Compared to most of the not-yet-shaving, not-yet-mature young guys crowded on board, I was a seasoned veteran of life. I hadn't really lived at home since age 14. Hitch hiking through Texas, I spent a night in jail when I couldn't explain my penniless presence one night on the streets of a shabby little town. The name of the town I had already forgotten. I didn't forget the experience and my vow never again to do anything that would put me behind bars, even overnight.

"Have you ever spent time in jail?" was one of the questions on my Navy enlistment papers. I felt duty bound to answer, "yes". Explaining the circumstances to the recruiting officer, he just laughed. They sure as hell were not going to let a minor flaw like overnight jail time rob them of an eager young recruit.

The train was slowing; creaking and groaning to a stop at one of those little towns snuggled into the sparsely populated Montana plains. The picture book station was straight out of an old Western movie and so were the leathered station workers exchanging shouted conversations with our train crew. Their every word was delivered in a cloud of steamy breath that left no doubt that this was winter time in cattle country.

Why were we stopping? Soon enough, I would learn that a condition of my enlistment was a surrender of all rights to know what the hell is going on.

Midnight was minutes away. A car full of young celebrants, couples, waited for the clanging, flashing signal to permit their crossing the tracks. From my perch inside the train, I could see the bottle being passed inside the car. This bunch was in no particular hurry. I would have made a pact with the devil to trade places with them. Enlistment was the first of my impetuous decisions from which there was no retreat. You get your life back when the Navy says so.

I wondered about the lives of all the citizens in this little town as our train lurched into forward motion. What was going on in those houses whose lighted windows and multi-colored Christmas lights reflected in the snow? Did they have a happy holiday season? Were some of the "men folk" off to war? Was there a fetching young girl who would have been eager to welcome me in if I could but escape this cattle train and knock on her door?

After agonizing days and nights, our train finally reached its destination. Less than 24 hours after checking into the sprawling training facility, I was minus my hair, my civilian clothes and my dignity. It was a bitter pill for this rebellious individual to swallow. The Navy would tolerate no rebellion, no individualism of any kind.

"Kamstra!" I got to shout out daily at 5 a.m. parade grounds muster. Except for that I was absolutely nobody. Everybody was nobody at Farrigut. This was a training camp for the shaved-head nobodies. From this day forward it was "fall in line and keep your mouth shut!" We learned to run, to march, to shoot, to use gas masks, to swim…and to obey orders without question.

Our drill instructors demanded our undivided attention daily. They briefed us on what fun things were on our day's schedule. As their shouting and screaming continued, their enjoyment in brow beating and terrifying young recruits became more obvious. They were actually getting off on this.

One day the mail from home included a note from my kid sister. She had seen my beloved "Blue Bomber" Ford tooling through town with a cream can-loaded rack welded on the back. Do the Auto Immunes of the world know no limit to the indignities they will heap upon a defenseless car? Some day I would own an even better machine. That was a dream, spiced with thoughts of home town girls, that would help me through these trying times.

"Fall in line and keep your mouth shut!"

AED heaven!

Brighter days were just ahead. My test scores spared me from the "report for immediate sea duty" most boot camp graduates had in store. I was selected for mechanics training at Great Lakes Naval Base, Chicago. Learning the inner workings of engines. Playing and puttering with things mechanical. I had survived the hell of Farrigut. This duty sounded like heaven for an AED addicted farm boy.

I wouldn't be working on – or driving – cars, but I would be surrounded by things mechanical. Refrigeration units, generators, evaporators, diesel engines, gas engines, boilers, pumps. AED heaven! My enthusiasm, plus an extra measure of dumb luck, took me from one advanced training school to another. I was seeing the eastern half of the U.S. and learning to be a truly knowledgeable AED addict. Graduation at one school involved reassembling a totally disassembled engine, then having it running before the time clock ran out. I graduated with clock time to spare. Loved that stuff!

Loved it but didn't forget that I had traded my home town freedom for some real battle action. There was a war on and I wanted to be part of it. Hiding out in Canada and other sneaky draft evasions were not part of the American culture in the 1940's. At least such activity would not have enhanced your chances of one day becoming president.

Finally, the Navy brass decided it was time for me to experience real shipboard life. In less than a year, I had gone from building ships to sailing on them. In Houston, Texas, the Navy not only built ships but simultaneously assembled their crews. Build-a-ship-build-a-crew; a real assembly line operation. One or two crew members knew about sailing; among the rest of us, most had never even seen the ocean.

Angry ocean, scared sailor

Then our ship was ready and we, the crew, were as ready as we would ever be. Enlisted men never knew where we were, where we were going or why. We had plowed through rolling seas from Houston to the Atlantic side of Florida. We were headed north. This night, experiencing the fury of an angry Atlantic Ocean, I was certain that my impatience to "get on with life" was about to cost me my life. I had "the duty" in the cramped engine room of a U.S. Navy ship, the LSM 113. The designation "LSM" was pragmatic Navy lingo for "Landing Ship Medium", meaning a medium sized landing ship that could ram itself onto a beach and disgorge tanks, guns and terrified troops.

Right now, we were in the Atlantic – submarine waters – somewhere off the east coast of the U.S. and we were running in a convoy without lights. "Running" for an LSM at full flank speed of 13 knots translated to about 15 miles an hour land speed. Faster warships, capable of more than twice our speed, had to reduce speed to our snail's pace. The bigger ships not only had speed, they had deep keels to slice through the heavy seas we were battling. An LSM keel, on the other hand, was mostly non- existent. More the configuration of a floating bath tub – with crew quarters inside the "walls" and below an open well deck – the LSM wallowed and pitched as it climbed over each wave and then came crashing down.

I didn't feel too good and I was scared as hell. The two Fairbanks Morse Diesels, putting out more than 1,000 horsepower each, screamed in my ears as I stood by the throttles. They screamed even louder each time the big propellers at the stern of the ship lifted out of the water as we descended another wave. The engine room was hot, deafening and an easy place to get sick especially if you were bothered by diesel fumes.

I usually got a kick out of cranking these big engines up to flank speed. Now it was obvious that any engine conceived by man was no match for a riled up ocean.

One of our seaman, secured by a line around his waist, held on for his life as he made his way across the deck of the LSM that seemed to stand on end each time it climbed to the top of another wave. His job: make instant spot welds

"A rage to live"

whenever he detected signs that deck seams were starting to open. For this the Navy paid him $30 a month plus "room and board".

It was hard to believe waves ever got so tall, higher than tall buildings. They crashed over us as though determined to send us to the bottom. My first time on the high seas and I prayed it would not be my last. Many of our novice crew were too sick and too terrified to function at all. We were a rag tag bunch. Guys from farms, from small towns and even one or two from the big city. Some were enlistees like me. Most were draftees, longing for wives and children left behind. At age 30, they were already "Old men" from my perspective.

Now, just turned 18, I was aboard ship, ready for what I was certain would be imminent contact with enemy forces. The ultimate adventure. Both the shipbuilding venture and the Navy enlistment were the direct result of a fire within me that I didn't fully comprehend yet. "A Rage To Live", some authors called it. I had a growing intolerance for the ordinary and the slow moving. Later, this would become the driving force behind a lucrative and soul satisfying career. At l6 and l7, however, it only triggered frequent impetuous decisions; decisions that could cost me my life or – maybe worse – turn its course to one of frustration and futility.

The latest such decision brought me to this nightmare night at sea. Former classmates were probably enjoying their senior prom this night. With envy and cursing my own stupidity, I envisioned these high school studs enjoying the ultimate in boy-girl relationships. And cars, cars, cars! Meanwhile, Ken Kamstra is bouncing around in an ocean-going bathtub intent on personally avenging the Japanese sneak attack on Pearl Harbor. I was obsessed with doing something extraordinary, something heroic .

"You're a lousy swimmer," the grizzled chief petty officer growled at me as he let me know in no uncertain terms that I would never make it as a Navy "Frog Man". I thought that elite corps of underwater saboteurs was a perfect match with my desire for heroic action. Second choice was the amphibious force. These were the guys who hit the beaches first in every invasion. And there were beach assaults happening everywhere in the South Pacific. Great! I was accepted and got to wear the gold shoulder patch with the ferocious alligator. My alligator, in fact had a jeweled eye, courtesy of the tailor who crafted my first form fitting "tailor mades". With broad shoulders, a 30 inch waste and a tiny tusch, I thought my new uniform was definitely the crowning touch. Such garb was strictly against regulation but it made me feel apart from the ordinary sailor.

As a teenager, of course, it had scarcely occurred to me that amphibious sailors were also among the first to die. Die with honor along with the troops charging off the LSM. But die nonetheless. If the Japs didn't get you the first time in, they would have more opportunities as you hit the beach again and again.

I thought only of the glory of it all. One of my high school buddies, a Marine, was slaughtered on the beaches of Iwo Jima. I doubt that he felt any sense of glory in his last seconds of life as the bullets ripped him apart.

So here I was at sea, undoubtedly headed for action that would fill my chest with ribbons and metals. When I came home on leave to Canby, those snooty girls who once snickered at my welfare-issue clothes would be proud to go out with me.

My engine room duty ended at 4 a.m. At 8 a.m., I awoke to a strangely calm sea. The sun was out. We were headed not for war but to Norfolk, Virginia. Seems the crew of the LSM 113 had performed so admirably that we were chosen to stay behind and train naval academy cadets, "rich kid" officers, in the art of amphibious warfare. How could this be! Weren't they aware that we had crashed into a Liberty cargo ship our first day at sea? Surely there must have been better performing crews than ours.

"You're a lousy swimmer"

It's Okay To Love Your Trailer Too – This One Even Has A Fan Club

1936. America was embarking on a touring, camping, vacationing boom. To fill the need for more trunk space, the Mullins Red Cap Utility Trailer was born. Its sleek art deco lines complemented the style of many mid-thirties cars.

Originals –now collectors vehicles – were only manufactured for two years; fiberglass reproductions followed. They are still popular today, seen behind restored collector cars and street rods, and at car shows across the country

Besides actual trailers, enthusiasts collect Red Cap cast iron toy trailers, literature and advertising. Restorers and fans exchange information through the Mullins Owners Club. Robert Parmelee, president of the Club, is also author of a new book, "Mullins Red Cap Utility Trailer: Handbook and History".

And who was the best performing, most outstanding crewman aboard the best performing LSM? Ken Kamstra, the farm kid from Canby, Minnesota.

They made me stay in my chair when my name was announced, however, and another sailor accepted the award. There wasn't time to change the award ceremony after they learned of my pending "Captain's Mast" disciplinary action. Something about refusing to obey an officer, a fracas about the cocky way I wore my hat that cost me 30 days of base restriction. Plenty of time to brood about not getting into the war. I hated the "trainee" officer who reported me; enjoyed making his kind puke as we taught them amphibious seamanship.

Damn! I cursed the cruel fate that kept me from action. Later, when the WWII body count was tallied, I became painfully aware of just how lucky I was to be still alive and possessed of a whole body. Hundreds of thousands of American GI's – many of them teenagers like me – were never coming home again. All the Kamstra brothers made it through the war unscathed. Even Hank, who fought his way across Europe with the infamous General Patton. Like Patton, sadly, it was a car crash, not battle, that killed Hank after the war.

Two years and four months later, the war was over and I was home, a tanned, trim 20-year-old looking for his future. I relished life's crossroads and turning points; so many options to ponder.

■ ■ ■

So many options…

CHAPTER 9

FREEDOM ISN'T FREEDOM
UNLESS YOU HAVE A CAR

It's a euphoric sense of freedom. Ken Kamstra, regulation-resisting maverick free! Free! Navy brass no longer in control of my life! Free to do as I damn well please. Go to bed when I want to; get up when I want to; do what I want to.

And I knew exactly what I wanted to do.

I drooled with AED anticipation

I wanted to get a car. No easy task when you only have what's left of $300 "mustering out" fund, now decimated by too many homecoming parties. What's more, car production was halted during the war. New cars were just coming back, but, pricewise, that was academic. Used cars were scarce and pricey, too. Oh to have my beautiful Blue Bomber back. My search of used car lots, random back yards, farm yards and more finally led me to a ratty old '38 Chevrolet in a small South Dakota town. It had seen better days; many, many better days. I negotiated the $50 price down to $40 and headed home, refilling the leaking, boiling radiator every few miles.

My parents had moved from Canby to Brookings, South Dakota, not far from my birthplace, a farm just south of town. Mom and Dad, now in their seventies, allowed as how I could live in a basement bedroom until I got my act together. I sometimes think their late life poverty was perpetuated by sons like me coming home to roost whenever we chose to. They seemed to genuinely welcome me, never complaining about my meager cash or work contributions.

Dad only grunted his disgust when I pulled up with my Chevrolet prize. It wasn't that the vehicle was an eyesore in his back yard, it was just that he still hated cars. I didn't converse as much with Dad as I later wish I had. He was deaf since childhood and I had to shout even in those rare times when he had his hearing aid turned up. Still we did communicate in our own way and I think we had a mutual respect.

Once I had watched my brothers reconstruct a wreck, now I would be the chief surgeon. I drooled with AED anticipation at the prospect of putting my intensive Navy training to personal use. In no time, I would have this old Chevy purring like the proverbial kitten and looking just as cute.

For the first time since early "teenhood", I faced each day with the happy prospect of passion for my work. Dad's beautiful oak tree was defiled with the attachment of my block and tackle device. Indispensable for an aspiring car surgeon about to perform a motor transplant. Then there was the matter of radiator repair, carburetor tune up, generator overhaul, new brakes and so on.

From time to time, my conscience nagged me to think about a real job. I considered one offer, operating heavy equipment for a construction company. Nah! That could get as boring as running diesel engines for the Navy. My lungs had absorbed enough of those stinking fumes to last a lifetime.

There was, of course, the "GI Bill", college tuition and meager stipend courtesy of Uncle Sam; gratitude for World War II service. One problem: I was short two years of high school. What the hell. One day I marched up to the Brookings High School principal's office.

"I want to finish high school," I announced. At six feet tall and a mature – I thought – 20, I probably didn't look much like a candidate for the junior class.

"You what?" gasped the principal. As we talked, he seemed to grow more sympathetic to my plight and we conversed at length. Finally, he said, "Ken, I think you should apply for admission to South Dakota State College. See if you can pass their entrance exams."

How am I going to do that with only two years of high school, I thought. Still, I thanked him. It was an intriguing idea, even exciting. I wondered, did I impress him with my demeanor? My vocabulary? I had learned mostly profanity in the Navy. What made him decide I should go directly to college?

Or did he catch me furtively ogling those cute girl students parading by his office? The sly devil! He was only protecting his vulnerable girls from a sailor who may have been at sea too long.

Whatever. I would give it my best shot. The college was across town, but only a few blocks from home. Still, I preferred to make my entrance – even if the college rejected me – by car rather than on foot. A few years at sea had only intensified my AED affliction.

■ ■ ■

"I want to finish high school"

My chariot was gleaming

My Chevy was still in the back yard intensive care unit. From the tree hung its rusty old six-banger. The timetable for completion would have to be speeded up if I was to make my grand entrance on the college campus. With new motivation, I reassembled the rebuilt engine, patched radiator, new wiring and more. A few days later, I hit the starter and the motor came clattering to life. Wow! Ken Kamstra was mobile again!

Not quite. Next the paint job. Sanding here. Dent pounding here. Then the paint. Black body, gaudy red wheels and big "hand painted" white sidewalls. To think that this old Chevy was facing an ignoble death in a junk yard. Now it would be bringing pure ecstasy to an AED addict overdue for therapy. I had to stand back and gloat. Dad walked by and actually patted me on the back. Didn't mean he had changed his mind about cars, but he appreciated dedicated effort. Besides, he was going to get his oak tree back.

■ ■ ■

My chariot was gleaming like a polished jewel when I made my grand entrance, pulling up in front of the college administration building. I lingered behind the wheel to drink in the drama of this new horizon of my life. Everywhere, students were scurrying to and from class or leisurely visiting in clusters.

I particularly noticed the girls. It was fall sweater weather and some of them did magnificent things for the common sweater. Most were farm girls or small town girls but that hadn't impaired their learning the fine art of dressing to emphasize bosoms and bottoms.

There was still the little matter of the college entrance exams. If I didn't pass, it would be years – if ever – before I could savor the life of higher education. The test took hours; the agony of waiting for results took forever. Finally the word came back.

Ken Kamstra has been accepted as a student at South Dakota State College.

I passed! I was now a bona fide college freshman. The life-seasoned kid from Canby was among the elite headed for higher learning. I should have rushed back to thank that high school principal for suggesting a direct route to college, but I didn't. His idea saved two whole years of my life, almost making up for the Navy years. Albeit with some outside help, impatience was again serving me well. To hell with high school; onward to college!

The Navy had turned me into a pretty good mechanic and a dead shot with a 50 caliber machine gun, but neither of these constituted preparation for college courses. Entrance exams identified law and English as my strongest aptitudes. I chose English and art. I loved words; thought I might have the makings of an artist as well. Then, like a kid in a candy store, I picked other courses at random: Shakespeare, criminology, anthropology, Spanish and more.

Art was fun and rewarding. My very first painting was put on display in a glass case just outside the college auditorium. Not only that, but there were far more girls than guys in the art classes.

■ ■ ■

A sailor's eye for bosoms and bottoms

CHAPTER 10

An AED Addict's Ultimate Dilemma: Win A Bride, Surrender Your Car

"Puritanical Forties"

I first noticed her in art class. Mimi, a pretty girl with dark brown hair. When the sun flooded into the aging classroom, red highlights in her hair were emphasized as the rays found just the right angle. I didn't think she made the most of that beautiful hair the way it was "done up", but what did I know. I knew she had absolutely great legs and the kind of fanny that could make any man lose his train of thought.

My train of thought in these art and design classes was mostly directed at all the girls anyway. It's what two plus years living aboard ship does to a guy. That's how I rationalized it anyway. Marriage was at least a decade away; meanwhile, what a fun decade it was going to be! Mimi had a trim, athletic build. To her credit, she dressed discreetly, not calling undue attention to her figure. Other girls – we could call them "girls" then – were shameless in emphasizing bosoms and other physical attractions. What healthy young male wouldn't enjoy their shamelessness.

Nonetheless it was still the "Puritanical Forties". Nude models in art classes, for instance, were unheard of. Instead, we were treated to a slightly overweight co-ed in a one piece bathing suit complete with front "skirt". Still a treat for a just-discharged sailor. Distractions not withstanding, I did create oil paintings the college chose to display. Should art be my chosen profession? I would think about it.

Not long after Mimi caught my eye in art classes, I saw her sitting with a girl friend at a "mixer" dance on campus. These affairs, I learned, were a tradition with Midwestern colleges; a way of facilitating a meeting of the sexes. Meeting was encouraged, mating was not. Policies that would be considered prim, primitive and downright repressive by succeeding generations were strictly enforced. Girls' dormitory rules required that boys go no further than the surgically-lit lobby. No heavy petting. All boys off premises by 10 p.m. Doors bolted and beds checked shortly thereafter.

Chastity ubber allus!

Mimi looked seductively chaste as I hesitantly approached her.

"May I have this dance?" I asked, feigning an air of nonchalance.

"Okay," she responded, blushing as she took my hand and let herself be led to the dance floor. So far, neither of us had demonstrated any sophisticated conversational skills. We weren't much better at dancing. Mimi later confessed to hating these kind of boy-meets-girl affairs. Her girlfriends had to drag her to this event.

Was this the fickle finger of fate?

I mumbled an apology for my dancing. The words were drowned out by the blaring band. I blamed the Navy for my clumsy dancing. Trying my best to sound worldly, I told Mimi that in "navy towns" along the east coast and in Guantanimo Bay – "Gitmo" – Cuba, the ratio of girls to sailors was about 1000 to 1. I had learned to hold my liquor but had little practice holding girls on the dance floor.

I doubt that she bought that.

With Mimi grasped awkwardly in my arms, I managed to bumble my way through a few dance numbers utilizing the one step I knew, all inclusive no matter what the band was playing. I called it my "two step". I don't know what Mimi and her friends called it after I – mercifully – returned her from the dance floor.

Preoccupied with my own uncooperative feet, I was nonetheless captivated by Mimi's striking hazel eyes. They seemed to take on an added sparkle as she talked about her kid brother and two younger sisters at home. Her family lived just 60 miles north of where we were saying our polite-but-wooden "thank you's" that ended our contact for the evening.

We only had a few minutes together, but there was a magnetism at work. Mimi was all softness and sincerity; I was all rough edges, a product of teenage independence, hard labor and military service. We couldn't have been more different.

> *There was magnetism at work*

> *My AED affliction was completely incomprehensible to her*

Some weeks after our casual dance encounter, I asked for a date: a movie with coffee following. Not lavish but even this much was stretching my meager funds. My GI living allotment was $65 monthly plus what I could earn at odd jobs. Somehow, 50 cents an hour had been established as the going pay rate for college student labor. It was better than no wages at all. I supplemented my GI money as a waiter, gas pump jockey, ditch digger and general laborer.

We continued dating. There were only occasional sparks initially. I remained confident of my no-marriage-for-ten-years pledge. But things were heating up. More and more, we just wanted to be together. Often we pretended that our mission was to study or maybe practice our Spanish lessons.

I liked the kissing and holding part best.

When Mimi arranged for me to meet her folks, I should have been wary. I was too busy stuffing my face. Her mother loved to cook; I loved to eat. Complete compatibility.

The inevitable happened. The word "marriage" was slipping into our conversations. Was my pledge of ten years of carefree bachelorhood slipping away? I considered taking off in the Chevy, leaving no forwarding address. But then some less deserving guy – probably a real jerk – would run off with Mimi. Thanks to my own rash actions, I had cheated myself out of my teen age freedom. Now it was time to enjoy some years without the responsibility of marriage or any other kind of obligation. Maybe go to France to study art. Maybe travel the country by car. Maybe who knows what.

Too often in my life, fate failed to step in and save me from unwise decisions. This time, love was becoming a stronger appeal than the call of carefree bachelorhood. Turning away from Mimi in favor of freedom at this junction, would have ranked as the ultimate stupidity of my life. Time would confirm the wisdom of following my heart. My AED affliction was completely incomprehensible to her but that was the only flaw I was able to detect.

We were becoming inseparable. The momentum was scary.

In no time, we found ourselves broaching the subject to her folks. I think they liked me well enough as just a boyfriend with a voracious appetite. A son in law was something else again. There was nothing in my credentials so far that would give them comfort that I could support their daughter. After all, I wasn't studying to be a doctor, lawyer, engineer or anything reassuring. I was instead taking a disjointed smattering of courses in art, English, criminology and anything else that intrigued me. Some compulsory courses, like Chemistry were beyond the scope of a high school drop out, but I got by. If Mimi's folks had asked me what profession or career I had in mind, I would have had to say, "I'm not sure just yet." Hardly reassuring for any protective parents.

"I think marriage is a dumb idea!"

These weren't their exact words. They were more tactful but that was the gist of their reaction. They thought we should finish or at least be further along in our education before we took the big step into marriage. Mimi was 19, I was 21.

As we contemplated marriage in spite of parental attempts at dissuasion, some realities hit home. Basics like, where would we live? No bride, no matter how much in love, should be asked to live in my damp, dingy basement quarters. Through the want ads, I found a used trailer house for $700. It would also solve another basic newlywed need, furniture. Trailer houses, even 18-footers, come with a bed, kitchen stove, sink, cupboards, table, oil heating stove, the works.

Problem: we didn't have $700. I usually had just enough money for the next tank of gas in my beloved Chevy.

My beloved Chevy! It finally dawned on me. Oh my God! If I wanted Mimi as my bride, I would have to sell the one possession dearest to my heart, my gleaming black Chevy! I had just recovered the seats and installed a spiffy new chrome spot light. This would be an agonizing, gut wrenching test of love. And what about my AED disease? Would my psyche be permanently impaired without my car? It was a dilemma no man should ever have to face.

"I think marriage is a dumb idea"

We had dodged the bullet

As I stood gazing at the Chevy, Mimi approached and put her arm around me; then we kissed. The Chevy had to go! An Auto Immune, Mimi would never fully understand, even though she did offer sympathy.

Carless and essentially penniless, we were married. It would be a life of sheer poverty; something old hat to me, but Mimi was yet to feel the full brunt of it.

After a nice low key wedding, we headed back to our cozy-but-dinky trailer home. Getting there strained my sense of manhood and my self esteem. We had to ask friends to drive us the 60 miles because we had no car. The absence of a car, a honeymoon or even a decent wedding ring were just some of the cashless realities of our new life together.

College classes started the next day. My college classes. Mimi would have to find work as a professor's secretary instead of continuing her studies. Things weren't all bleak; our wedding night was at hand.

The hand of fate almost made it our first and last night together.

Just to make things extra cozy, I lit the tiny oil heater that represented the "heating system" for our home. Then we went to bed. Sometime during the night, we smelled smoke. Almost before we could react, the trailer home filled with thick black smoke. The heater, it turned out, was leaking oil onto the trailer house floor, starting a smoldering fire. Had we been soundly sleeping, smoke inhalation undoubtedly would have killed us in our sleep.

I was out of bed and to the scene of the fire in one leap, Mimi at my heels. Nude and crouched beside the trailer, I threw dirt onto the smoldering floor until the fire was smothered. We had dodged the bullet. Next, we aired out the trailer; then did what any red blooded newlyweds would do. We went back to bed.

Next day, I began my second year of "general science" studies. "General science" is college-speak for "this guy still doesn't know what he wants to do when he grows up". The government had upped my $65 monthly stipend to $95, the amount designated for a married student. To supplement our meager income, I worked as a gas station attendant, waiter, janitor and, as always, general

Check your guns

laborer. Even tried my hand – being a budding artist and all – at painting signs. The restaurant owner was thrilled with my work and my cheap rates. Right up until he discovered I had misspelled "Stolpenopolis".

Our first Christmas together was marred by the realization that our income was far short of our basic needs for survival. The government made things worse by stopping subsistence payments during holidays when classes were not in session.

Soon after the holidays, I found a job. Eating had to take precedence over education. The job included board and room. In a remote prairie town, I would be managing a dormitory for high school boys and girls. Kids who lived so far from school that the state arranged for a dormitory that included bed and board. The board was provided by two local women who loved to eat as much as they loved to prepare generous, "rib sticking" meals. Mimi, of necessity already an expert at stretching multiple meals from a single can of Spam, shared my glee at the prospect of unlimited food.

Boys and girls came to this little South Dakota town from distant farms and ranches. Among my disciplinary responsibilities: make students check in their guns before starting the week. Decades later, school gun checks would be commonplace, but this was the Forties and these guns really were for random hunting and not for popping other students. Disarming the students was far easier than keeping the boys and girls in their separate sleeping quarters.

The job ended with the school year. And in the years immediately following, I would try my hand at a wide range of employment. The selections were as limited as my education. Most jobs provided little more than "food on the table". Food for my starving ego had to come from my unwavering conviction that somewhere out there was a soul-satisfying, money-making career with my name on it.

■ ■ ■

CHAPTER 11

LEARN TO DRIVE AND THERE ARE NO LIMITS

Hard driving

It's 5 a.m., a time of day when you can almost imagine you aren't sharing the Minneapolis-St. Paul "Twin Cities" with more than a million other inhabitants. This is one of those perfect spring mornings that are occasionally bestowed upon Minnesotans emerging from their long winter siege.

There is just enough breeze to waft the scent of apple blossoms over the open cockpit of my Ferrari.

I've nosed the ferocious little beast under the overhanging branches of the nearest crabapple tree. Just beyond the flower laden tree is a thing even more beautiful to me. It's a low slung black-and-brass sign that reads: KAMSTRA CENTER. It identifies a sprawling complex of interconnected, stone buildings nestled among apple, pine and birch trees and sitting on a four-acre carpet of rolling, manicured lawn.

The sun reflects in the glass. I reflect on a career search that once seemed futile. In time, I learned it wasn't a career I should have been seeking; a career suggests a course of action predetermined and just waiting for someone to get in step. The object of my quest should have been a special capability; applicable anywhere, rewarding, satisfying and – most important – without limitation.

My capability: driving. Hard driving.

No, not just 200-miles-per-hour Ferraris – that's AED therapy – but driving life itself. Making the most of that God given capability and enjoying just about every minute of it.

"My own advertising agency!" I am embarrassed saying this aloud. It sounds like a line from a third rate movie. In a way, it is like a movie, but a good one. An epic adventure starring an undereducated farm kid who came to the big city to seek his fortune. It is a highly improbable tale: me giving advice to Fortune 500 clients who market their products worldwide. Kamstra Communications, headquartered in St. Paul with an office in Texas and a joint venture in London, England. Good God!

There are fortunes and there are successes that easily dwarf mine. But none could be any sweeter.

I sit snuggled in the hand stitched leather seats of the in-your-face-red Ferrari and gaze with unabashed pride and self satisfaction at the new Kamstra headquarters. The satisfaction is all the sweeter knowing that I paid cash (plus tax; see next page) for the new Ferrari and that every dollar that went into it and the state-of-the-art new offices were earned by me. Earned the hard way, one dollar at a time.

I am a driver.

It is a truly joyous state of mind and state of being. No drug could ever deliver the sustained euphoria of driving your own destiny. Add to this the sheer, almost orgiastic pleasure of driving fast cars fast and you begin to wonder if you haven't figured out what life is all about.

Most people think of drivers in the work place as domineering, insensitive slave drivers. Not so. Slave drivers are just what they appear to be, egotistical asses. A genuine driver leads by inspiration and by highly sensitized insights into the motivational forces at work in the people chosen to help achieve each goal. Driving is about 16 hour days and 100 hour weeks; about seeing a dream so clearly that you seldom see the clock.

My life is about the gentle art of helping people – both staff and clients – connect to their own driving force and then to experience the thrill of making things happen. Business, I have learned, is about people. In a few more hours, the fifty-plus people who make things happen for their clients, their agency and themselves will be arriving at Kamstra Center. Others will be starting their day at Kamstra Communications in Austin, Texas. Employees of our joint venture offices in London are already well into their day.

I will be long gone before our U.S. staff arrives for work. I have selected this day for an emotional – and, yes, egotistical – mission. Finding my life's purpose and then relentlessly pursuing it has been a long and arduous journey. It has also been all consuming. If there was a threshold over which I stepped to join the ranks of achievers, I missed it. It could have happened on one of those days when I and my staff were working around the clock to meet a client's deadline.

Kamstra Center, a driver's improbable dream

A Ferrari mission

This day I had set aside as "by-God-I've-done-it day". There had to be a benchmark, a milestone, a time to savor success before going back into the game.

I would retrace the starting points of the journey that eventually brought me to this glorious day. I couldn't retrace it all: work that took me to New York, New Orleans, Dallas, San Francisco, London. Rare vacation trips to Paris, Rio de Janeiro, Buenos Aires, Santiago and more. Mind boggling adventures for a kid who grew up without television, telephones, electricity, plumbing or any concept of what the rest of the world was all about. The journey, for now at least, would be confined to Minnesota and South Dakota. Where it all began.

By now, hopelessly AED addicted to cars – preferably fast cars – I saved many of them. After all, each had played their part in my life's journey. The Auto Immune majority would never understand, but each car had earned a position as part of the Kamstra family. One just didn't cast them aside simply because they were growing old. Kamstra Center was in fact constructed with five snugly safe and warm basement parking spaces for "Ken's cars." Preparing for this day, I carefully chose the right vehicle for the occasion. Should it be my first BMW, a 1974 3.0 coupe or maybe the big 12-cylinder 850i BMW coupe? The sleek 928 Porsche, only 15 years old, was a tempting tourer. So was the 1969 Mercedes 280.

Nope.

This was definitely a Ferrari mission. It was time to go. I fired up the Ferrari and swung out of the Kamstra Center parking lot, indulging myself in one last look at the handsome stone structures.

The joy I feel as the morning air engulfs me is tempered by a growing awareness. Unrelenting forces are working to declare my achievements to be little more than monuments to greed and avarice. Liberal proponents of this "Mediocrity Movement" brand entrepreneurial success repugnant and politically incorrect. Their social engineering theories would be further shattered if they were to learn the ugly truth about Ken Kamstra. I had, after all, succeeded without government subsidy and in spite of growing up in poverty and dropping out of high school. Freedom to excel, they are convinced, must be prevented at any cost. After all, what will happen to the fragile self esteem of under achievers if we permit some people to attain more success than others?

"My Ferrari will be the first to go under this new social – socialist – order", I think to myself as I hear the growling of 300 thirsty horses pushing us onto the freeway. I press the gas pedal ever so gingerly, mindful of the go-slow-Gestapo who would love to start their day with a Ferrari trophy. The guttural sounds of this magnificent machine find their way into my soul and my psyche. Soon I am off the freeway and onto the backroads for which Ferrari's were created.

"Screw you, Mr. Clinton! Screw all the government intrusion you would foist upon this great nation!" By your socialist party policies, the exhaust from my Ferrari is more harmful to America than your sexual escapades in the Oval Office.

How can I be enraged and elated and the same time, I ask myself, instantly aware that both emotions have found their way to my right foot. The Ferrari's orange-on-black speedometer reads 110 and climbing. I back off. I will not be a trophy this day.

We are cruising now, this beautiful Ferrari and I. Me, the machine and five gated gears in perfect synchronization, lusting for hills and curves to challenge us. At times, the feisty Ferrari engine shatters the morning stillness with its joyous screams as I downshift at every opportunity. I wonder about people who prefer "practical" cars with automatic transmissions. Do they ever yearn to actually participate in the driving process or are they forever content just to steer their sound deadened marshmallows?

They at least will have less to lament if Al Gore succeeds in converting us to a carless society. I wonder about Al Gore. He's got kids so he must have had sex. But did he actually enjoy it? Did he change expression at the moment of climax? I doubt it.

My profound pondering is halted by an orange triangle dead ahead. Slow moving vehicle. A bronzed young boy driving a tractor is blocking my forward progress and not particularly concerned about my inconvenience. Over the noise of his rig, he hears the Ferrari's growl of protest as we gear down to

I will not be a trophy this day

Suckloot

Suckloot loves your car as much as you do; maybe even more. When you get that "Honey-we-need-a new-car" glint in your eye, Suckloot starts to drool. You envision a sleek new chariot; he sees a fat golden goose. He finds comfort envisioning himself feeding on it, sucking sustenance from it. The tax banquet, he knows, will go on every day you own it. Pig out time starts when your car dealer presses those new car keys into your trembling hands. The lavish, ever-expanding menu includes such delights as: state sales tax, city sales tax, luxury tax, gas guzzler tax, license tax, gas tax, emission-testing tax and much, much more. Suckloot is one of the oldest and best fed of all Cargoyles. He's been on the automotive scene since Grandpa first chugged into the driveway with his new Model-T. He'll be around after you're gone – collecting taxes on any cars left in your estate. Cargoyles are forever.

■ ■ ■

*You bought a car
like some rich dude?
Why then we'll tax
your attitude.*

*We'll tax each gallon
that you burn.
'Tis Mother Earth
that's our concern.*

maybe 5 miles per hour. The kid looks over his shoulder at me and my toy. It is more a look of disdain than admiration or envy.

"What's that old fart doing in a sports car?", he's probably thinking.

It makes me feel defensive. I want to straighten him out.

"Look, you young punk", I want to say, "I know about cars. I have driven them on race tracks. Once, before they got computerized and complicated, I could tear an engine apart and put it back together again. I'm not trying to recapture my youth; I never let it get away. I will be young and I will be hard driving right into eternity!"

Get hold of yourself, Kamstra, this is Minnesota farm country and these are your kind of people. They're free and filling their lungs with fresh air every day while you're stuck in your fancy city offices. They are your kind of people, Ken, its just that they really don't give a damn about you right now; they've got a crop to get in. Like you, they get up before the sun and get at it.

I content myself with dodging pickup trucks and farm machinery for the rest of the morning as a I make my way across the rolling southwestern Minnesota farm country. Slowing down and regaining speed gives me added opportunity to orchestrate the Ferrari's clutch, gas peddle and gear box.

Besides, these are probably some of the most beautiful and serene surroundings to be found anywhere on earth. One wouldn't want to miss it no matter how much fun it is to drive fast. I've seen a good bit of the world and I believe these country dwellers really know where to live as well as how to live. Youngsters like the boy on the tractor probably can't wait to get away and see the world. They will have to learn as I did that "the world" is more a state of mind. Right now, my state of mind plasters a big silly grin across my face. This is one helluva' lot of fun!

Ignoring road signs – and speed limits whenever possible – I make my way south and west. Destination: Canby, Minnesota. Canby, my first taste of "city life", fifth grade through high school sophomore; at which time I decided "enough education already!" Enroute, we cruise through Marshall, Ghent,

This is one helluva' lot of fun!

Minneota, Taunton, Porter. Each presents opportunities for more gear box symphonies; the magnificent Ferrari engine alternately screaming and growling as I slow and then accelerate. These are the "nowhere towns" where I learned serious beer drinking, girl-chasing and other teen age misbehavior.

It's mid morning in Canby. Farmers and city dwellers are going about their daily routines that have changed little in the decades since this was my home town.

Here I am making my triumphant return to the scene of my uneventful youth and nobody notices. Ferraris cause little stir in Minnesota farm towns. Most folks don't know – or care – what in hell you're driving. I cruise the streets. A new Canby High School had been erected. The old one, shabby and run down even in my day, still stands next to it. Students meander out of the building, exuberant in their horse play.

Even in my Ferrari, I feel like a dinosaur returned to earth,

Next stop, my old house on the wrong side of town. It's been torn down to enlarge the neighbor's lawn. Where is their respect for history and nostalgia? I take a picture of the street and the street sign. Sixth and Ring Streets.

On to the Depot Cafe. There is no depot in Canby anymore, but freight trains still rumble through, mostly hauling grain and corn. The cafe is where the depot used to be; so it's the Depot Cafe. Time for lunch and some nostalgia talk with my older brother, Les. While most of the 11 Kamstra's sought their fortunes in other states, Les stayed close to home. Now he was "Professor Kamstra" at South Dakota State College just across the border in Brookings. Brookings, the little college town where my "higher education" ended almost before it began. A town that was my birthplace; where I found a bride but couldn't find work.

We finish an early lunch. Just about everybody at the Depot has the hot beef sandwich special. So do we. Then out to the parking lot. Les immediately notices my new convertible with its "prancing horse" grill.

"Hey, a new Mustang. Hot damn!"

"Hey, a new Mustang. Hot damn!"

Old home, new Ferrari

Les was one of the Auto Immune. Cars were just something that took you from point A to Point B. I could've explained that it was a Ferrari with a fat, six figure price, but why bother. Les just wasn't into cars except for the pickup trucks he always drove. He was, after all, a biochemist in a farm area college. But we still had rapport: the ad huckster and the professor.

Off to our old farmstead we went. Enroute, we would swap time-worn stories about growing up on the farm, the one-room school and all that. I told him about this my "special day" and I think he understood. But his was a well ordered, logical life; mine wasn't.

In less than 15 minutes, we were roaring down the dusty road to our old farm home. It looked forlorn perched on a slight rise in the surrounding, flat-as-a-pancake farmland. This was our annual ritual. The barn is still standing. The tool shed – next to which my brothers resurrected the "flying Ford" – was

gone. But not the memory. Everyone has at least one childhood memory that stays with them forever. I had many, but none as strong as the day I learned – on this old Kamstra farm – the euphoric thrill of fast driving.

We linger, enjoying the bittersweet pleasure of reminiscing. Then it is time to go; Les to his home; me to complete the journey.

■ ■ ■

Just across the Minnesota border into South Dakota, I slam the gas pedal all the way down. The Ferrari, as impatient with dawdling as I have been, responds with a bellow. Then it settles in to that lovely, muffled this-is-more-like-it sound. A sound only Ferrari's make. The sound finds its way into my solar plexus and at once we are again in heavenly synchronization, Just me and the Mondial Ferrari heading west. Top down. Foot down. Flying!

Incurable car freaks like me will contrive any excuse to get behind the wheel and drive somewhere. South Dakota has always been my favorite somewhere. The fact that it is "fly over" land to most Americans – a place they would prefer not to be caught dead in – only enhances its appeal to me. In this state, there are only nine people, nice unpretentious people, for every square mile of land. Room to let a car out the way God meant for cars to be driven. Room to breath and feel free.

South Dakota is where I was born, number 12 of 13 farm kids to bless and burden the lives of Martin and Annie Kamstra. Its where they were laid to rest, probably the only real rest they ever knew.

Ahead, nearly centered in the state was the town of Huron, home of my "alma mater", the *Daily Plainsman* newspaper. Today's mission was to re-examine life from "plainsman" perspectives, to reconnect, recharge my batteries. My memory cells start working overtime as I think of the patient people who helped me get the hang of newspaper work. I probably never thanked them enough.

I feel adrenaline pumping as the Ferrari gobbles up road and we approach reconnect.

■ ■ ■

My adrenaline pumps as the Ferrari eats road

CHAPTER 12

L LIFE SKILLS TAUGHT HERE

"It looks mighty dead"

It was an act of absolute immaturity but I had to do it. I "rapped the pipes" on the Ferrari as I made the sweeping curve that took me over the sleepy James River and into Huron. Indulging in reminiscence, I was again the Ken Kamstra of l952, piloting my lime-green-and-black '49 Ford V8 coupe with its twin pipes making magnificent, pulsating exhaust sounds.

One of the beauties of carrying the AED gene is that you can find excuses, driving excuses, to "visit your past". Nothing is ever the same, of course, but you can restimulate memories. This day, I was remembering how – after an ill timed Korean War Navy hitch – I came to Huron hoping this would not be still another false career start

On this revisit, I tried to be the casual, big city sophisticate as I turned onto the "main drag" west into Huron. In spite of my resolve, though, that corny feeling of the triumphant returning hero came over me. I relished cruising the familiar streets of Huron. A few teenage heads turned as my red Ferrari rumbled by. Most adults didn't care diddley what kind of wheels I had. The younger ones didn't know Ferrari from Toyota. They only knew that in a more just world they, not me, would be driving that sexy red convertible.

I wasn't here to show off my car; I was here to reconnect with some very important personal history. It is said that opportunities are never labeled as such. Certainly, Huron could have inspired that truism.

"It looks mighty dead, "was my impression of the town when I first arrived decades ago. "It looks even deader" was my reaction as I revisited the place now. Still, I had a special affection for Huron. "Unlabeled" as a seat of opportunity, it could be said it was actually disguised. Yet, here in this "dead" town I finally connected with that elusive job that had my name on it.

"The old *Plainsman* headquarters will be moved out to some damn industrial park and squeezed into a dumpy cement block rectangle somewhere," I grumbled to myself.

I was wrong. The old *Daily Plainsman* was right where it always was for the last half century or more. Narrow, store front, red brick structure right down town where it belonged. Three stories tall. Still the bastion of order and nerve center for news in these parts.

I eased myself out of the tight confines of the Ferrari and stood for a moment gazing at the *Daily Plainsman* headquarters. Decades ago, when I stood at this very same spot, I lacked both confidence and cash. Still, I felt certain that something good was about to occur in my young life.

Just weeks before my job interview in Huron, I had traveled to Newfoundland, courtesy of the U. S. Navy. What a poetic twist of fate that Huron would become my own "new-found-land", a place where I would develop lasting, growing capabilities. Life skills.

■ ■ ■

Huron, a place as seemingly dead and desolate as Argentua, Newfoundland. The Navy, for reasons an amphibious-trained machinists mate was not allowed to know, sent me there to do my part in what was known as the "Korean Conflict". At 27, I was already a "double veteran" of World War 11 and Korea. Seems I had developed a certain level of competence in the operation of engines and equipment aboard amphibious landing craft. It was a dubious and dangerous specialization, one for which I had unwittingly volunteered in a fervor of patriotism fueled by the Japanese bombing of Pearl Harbor. I was only 17 then. What did I know.

Two wars before age 30. Can this be fair? No, it all has to do with being born at the wrong time. Here the author gets leave time from the "Korean Conflict". And quality time with daughter, Linda, and her mom. Some AED time, too, with the Kamstra's aging '40 Buick.

But this day in 1952 I was a civilian again. Dressed – over dressed as it turned out – in my only suit and an almost spotless red tie. The surprised receptionist at the *Daily Plainsman* stifled a snicker when I announced myself as an applicant for the news reporter's job. She directed me upstairs. Making my way up, I could hear laughter from the first floor. I didn't need embarrassment on top of growing panic.

Wow! Real newspaper people

The narrow stairway led to a newsroom crammed elbow to elbow with staffers. Most had phones cradled between shoulder and ear as they typed furiously whatever news they were extracting from their phone conversations. Wow! Real newspaper people, I thought. Behind me in the narrow reception area was a glass-enclosed cage with two teletype machines clattering away, spewing out news on continuous rolls of paper. I watched, mesmerized, waiting for someone to acknowledge my presence.

"I'm Bruce Campbell. Can I help you?"

He was a big guy, just slightly overweight. But then, everybody seemed overweight to me as I stood there, tall and skinny, feeling dumb, overdressed and on stage before the shirt-sleeved newsroom crew.

"I'm here to see about the news reporter job," I stammered. The news staff made a pretense of not listening. "My name is Ken Kamstra," I added, remembering that I had forgotten to give that vital piece of information.

"Oh yes, I've been expecting you," Bruce replied," let's go downstairs and have a look at your resumé," he said, getting up from his cluttered desk.

"My God!" I thought, "I don't have a resumé; I'm not sure I can even spell resumé and I don't know how to type either". Most of the time, I didn't miss the education I had skipped. Right now I missed it something awful.

Panic increased with each step as I followed Bruce downstairs. At least I wouldn't have to fall on my face in front of the newsroom crew. But what the hell would I say? I didn't have a resumé. I did have one helluva' wide range of experience: Navy machinist, Great Lakes ore boat fireman, Jewel Tea door-to-door salesman, insurance salesman, auto body shop apprentice, shipyard electrician and a few other jobs I couldn't remember in my growing terror. "Directionless" between two wars, I had taken some college English courses. Maybe Bruce would be impressed with that.

Like any man about to die, my whole life – at least my working life – was flashing before me as we descended the stairs.

I didn't like what I saw. Neither did Bruce Campbell. He saw little that would cause him to believe that I could ever be a newspaper reporter,

"For God's sake, you can't even type! "he groaned like a man in true agony. "What in hell are you going to do; have us wait around while you write out your stories long hand?"

"I'll learn to type", I answered meekly, realizing I was about to blow this job opportunity if I didn't do better and do it fast. I wasn't completely sure why, but I knew I was meant for this job. I had to have it. I would not be turned away. Over and over, I tried to emphasize the value of my college English courses. I even tried to attribute worth to my "varied" work history.

Shamelessly, I appealed to his sense of patriotism: "I'm a veteran of two wars!" I blurted out. "I have a wife and daughter to feed."

I was almost begging now and I didn't like myself for it. This was Ken Kamstra who took no shit nor sympathy from any man. But I had to have this job!

Finally, more out of exhaustion than conviction, Bruce relented.

"Okay, I'll put you on probation for 90 days", he said. Then, thinking, added, "but if you don't work out, that's it!"

It had been a long and grueling session and we were both a bit worn by it. I couldn't have been more elated if he had just made me editor in chief. I shook hands with as much business like dignity as I could muster. I really wanted to shout for joy and maybe do cartwheels over the desks of the smart asses in the business office who had snickered as I introduced myself.

"Oh, and learn to type," Bruce called after me.

Bruce's parting admonition brought me back to earth, but only for an instant. I hit the street and bounded for my "Newscruiser", glass packs rumbling, heading north to Watertown and the dingy basement apartment that had been the family abode ever since the Korean recall. Notorious government spending was not in evidence with my recall. It arrived by postcard, unceremoniously

"Oh, and learn to type"

telling me to get my ass back in Navy uniform. Whenever I was tempted to pity myself for this indignity and disruption in my life, I had but to think of the 35,000 GI's whose lives were permanently ended by the war. Suddenly, my inconvenience seemed rather trivial.

But this was a triumphant return. Now, I was ready to forge ahead.

First step was to rent a typewriter. The best I could do was a tiny pink portable obviously meant for more delicate fingers than mine. It was a malevolent monster in spite of its prissy pink exterior. With typing instruction book at my side, I pounded away at "the quick brown fox" and other exercises guaranteed to transform the unskilled. The pink demon fought me every step of the way, locking up its keys and defying me to untangle them.

"My God!" I blurted out one night, certain that some vengeful force had willed this machine on me to stymie my journalistic career before it ever got off the ground. I kept at it through the weekend, then took the willful little beast with me to my one-room living quarters in Huron.

The pace of the place as I took my assigned spot in the newsroom Monday morning was hard to comprehend. Phones were ringing constantly. Most were answered by staffers simultaneously listening, talking and typing. My first assignment was to get the facts from city hall on a revised dog ordinance. Not front page stuff to be sure but I wanted to compose the piece with absolute perfection. I had managed to get down the first two sentences on my adult sized typewriter when Bruce leaned over my laborious efforts.

"You'll just have to compose your stories faster! Do it in your head while you are driving back to the newsroom for Christ's sake!"

Bruce, mostly a patient and helpful boss, was losing it as he stood over my typewriter.

"It's not the composing, it's getting the hang of this typewriter," I said, at once realizing I was making matters worse. Bruce and the newsroom staff didn't need to be reminded that the new guy couldn't even type much less know anything about news reporting.

"Compose your stories faster!"

Bill Plummer made matters still worse. Plummer, news wire editor, decided which stories went where, how long they would be and what the headline should say. He had only hours to get the first daily edition on the press by noon.

Minutes were crucial!

Bill ripped stories off the Teletype machines and converted all or parts of them to stories for the *Daily Plainsman*. He also ripped stories from reporters' typewriters. Some twenty years of news writing and editing had imbued him with an uncanny ability to comprehend the gist of a story and its relative importance as it was coming to life in any Teletype or typewriter.

Without warning, he stepped up to my typewriter and began to tear off the top part of my story.

"Wait!" I pleaded. "I don't know where I am going with that story yet."

"I know where I am going with it", Bill said with an unsympathetic chuckle and headed back to the composing room with the first paragraph of my very first news story. It was a lesson I would not forget. Know where you are going with a story before you sit down to write it and forget about the luxury of "massaging" your priceless prose. That's not the way a daily newspaper works. Think fast. Write even faster. Get it right the first time.

Retrieving your copy from Bill's waste basket was not an option either. Bill used the basket as his spittoon. You didn't want to go fishing through it.

Bill and others in the "back room" jockeyed the stories and pictures until each page was composed – in lead "slugs" set in trays; not computer screens – to their satisfaction. Everything must be in balance and, most important, on time.

Novices like me upset this balance.

Bruce, however, was the stabilizing influence at the *Plainsman*. Unflappable, untiring, precise and professional, Bruce Campbell made everything and everybody work. A veteran newsman, Bruce Campbell, was my mentor. He and Bill were thrust into the role, but they handled it admirably.

Novices like me upset the balance

Kind of a mental shorthand

A few weeks into this mentoring process – but long before my probation was up – I moved Mimi and daughter Linda to Huron with me. We found our new apartment, the entire upstairs floor of a delightful old home on the edge of downtown. What's more, the landlady was a nice as her home. She became a friend. A refined, educated widow, she was always ready to chat and now and then invited us to dinner. Mimi loved the place. And she loved the "place" I had found in the pulse of the city…and in our own world.

What my bosses instilled in me, I was later to realize, would be invaluable to me every day of my life. They taught me to see, to listen, to observe, to ask questions, to perceive. Most significantly, they taught me to quickly and precisely interpret what this probing and observing process brought forth.

"Life skills taught here" should have been a sign in the *Plainsman* window.

In the months that followed, I found myself unconsciously and automatically separating the relevant from the seemingly irrelevant as news sources responded to my questions. Answers coming from their lips were instantaneously stripped of extraneous verbiage, then simultaneously reconstructed by me without disrupting the questioning process. It was a kind of mental short hand.

Exhilarating was not a strong enough word to describe my reaction to what was happening inside my head. I would not have believed that the human brain – at least my brain – could process information this fast. Best of all, the speed seemed to increase accuracy rather that hamper it.

"Everyone in the world should get their basic training at the *Daily Plainsman*," I thought as my learning progressed. Nonetheless, the daily challenge was still to find news equal to what I felt was my growing journalistic prowess.

One fact was obvious. A generous quantity of curiosity and imagination was an unwritten prerequisite for the job. The beat, after all, was a town where very little news was happening. Cynics might say that absolutely nothing was happening. My day began with a leisurely stroll to the police headquarters just two blocks down from the *Plainsman*.

"Morning, Harry," was my daily greeting to the beefy, aging desk sergeant. His cage was surrounded by wood and glass that partially hid the clutter inside.

"What's happening?" I would ask and Harry's response was almost always the same.

"Nothin' much, Ken; been a quiet night and looks like a slow day."

Harry liked it that way. For me it meant another tough challenge to find some news to write about. He was painfully right of course. There wasn't a hell of a lot going on. The police blotter I was permitted to peruse revealed an absence of any excitement. A couple of drunks locked up for their own best interests and one fender bender.

Hell. How can a guy fill a newspaper this way?

"Wait just a darn minute!" I say to myself, "that fender bender could be interesting. "

I try to squeeze more details out of old Harry. Harry loves to talk and spin yarns but he clams up if its anything the police don't want the press to know. He and the chief are still chafing over the *Plainsman's* legal victory allowing them to monitor police radio in the newsroom

"What's this about somebody running their car into an outhouse?" I ask.

"Oh, just the town drunk," says Harry.

"Was anybody in the biffy when it happened?"

"Just some kid, I understand, but he wasn't really hurt or anything." Harry responds, obviously tiring of my grilling.

I write down the names of those involved and head back to the newsroom before Harry gets his nose out of joint. I smell a story here, no pun intended. The incident took place in a little town of about 100 people just east of Huron. I call the owners of the home at the accident scene. The lady answering the phone is flustered but friendly as plains folks usually are. Seems that she and

"I smell a story here"

"Inside The Toilet Was Crumley"

her husband are playing host to their nephew from New York City. He's just 12 and thoroughly enjoying the fresh air and home cooking on the South Dakota prairie. He's not too crazy about outdoor toilets but he adapts. Outhouses are, of course, an integral part of the prairie landscape. On the evening in question, he was making what he hoped would be his last visit to this primitive "two hole" facility before turning in for the night.

He hadn't figured on the town drunk.

Weaving about the unpaved streets of this little village, the drunk finally lost control and crashed – you guessed it – into the outhouse. The outhouse was tipped over with the terrified New Yorker still inside. Only his pride was hurt. To make matter worse, but better for me, the young man's name was Crumley. Somehow, it seemed a name well suited for such a hapless young man.

"Inside The Toilet Was Crumley," read the punch line of my story.

Small town, small paycheck; big names

Bruce, Bill and everyone in the newsroom enjoyed the story. Bill gave it a "box" position on the front page. Both the AP and UP wires carried the story nationally. Crumley's misadventure had made my day.

Curiosity and imagination. The more I honed them the more stories I began to discover all around me. One day, not long after the outhouse story, Bruce took me aside and offered me my own "by line" column. We called it "City Sidelights", rather pretentious for a town of 15,000 inhabitants that didn't really constitute a city. For me, however, it was Ego City. There was no increase in pay, but Bruce no longer brought up my probation either.

There was more to the job than making national stories from outhouse incidents. I covered my first suicide, seeing up close what a shotgun blast does to the human head. I learned the intricacies of legal trials wherein I had to treat both defense, prosecution and the judge's rulings with equal fairness. If I failed, I would hear about it; this was a small town and there was no such thing as journalistic anonymity.

It was a small town but I met and interviewed "big" people. Hubert Humphrey – one day to be U.S Vice President – was a regular. We even did a radio news show together. I interviewed world famous clown Emmet Kelley and Rocky Marciano and Jack Dempsey and Arthur Godfrey. One day, Eleanor Roosevelt came to town.

■ ■ ■

CHAPTER 13

THE WINDS OF CHANGE;
AN INTERVIEW WITH ELEANOR

Utopia without cars? Get real!

Eleanor Roosevelt hung onto to her hat; I grasped her hand and together we made our way from her plane to the wood frame building that passed for an airport facility just north of Huron. Most every day is "wind swept" in central South Dakota, but this day was a real bitch kitty. It must have been tricky bringing the big Braniff plane into that tiny airport. No room for pilot error.

Eleanor was bringing with her the proverbial "winds of change"; barnstorming America to further the new social order that had been fashioned by her late husband, Franklin Delano Roosevelt, over a history-making, four-term presidency

The government-funded Utopia that the Roosevelts espoused would one day include a 55 miles-per-hour national speed limit and, ultimately, an all out campaign to rid the world of all vehicles with internal combustion engines. But this was 1953, and neither Eleanor nor I could have foreseen the coming totality of "Roosevelt-hood" in America.

To this gracious and tireless lady, whose life had been laced with the comforts and privileges of wealth, Huron must have seemed the middle of nowhere. In a way, it was. Major media types didn't bother to show for her arrival, and local dignitaries suddenly got stage fright; too awed to step forward. So I did. I was – ahem – the city editor of the Huron *Daily Plainsman* and Eleanor was, after all, the former first lady of the United States. Somebody had to escort her from her plane.

Beards were not in fashion then, but I was wearing a full one in preparation for a coming state celebration. The beard probably confirmed her suspicions that this was, indeed, the wild and primitive west. Teddy Roosevelt knew the Dakotas from personal, life-threatening experience. Eleanor didn't.

"It's so nice to be in your city. How are the crops doing this year?" Eleanor was trying to make conversation as we braced into the wind.

"Looks like a great year; plenty of rain." I shouted back. Actually, I had little knowledge about the crops, but it seemed like the right thing to say. We both realized the futility of trying to hold a conversation while gulping in mouthfuls of Dakota soil and walked the rest the way in silence.

"What would you care about our crops, anyway," I thought to myself. "You have your New York mansion at Hyde Park; my dad farmed this land for a lifetime and never made a dollar he could keep." But that was class envy talk. Truth was, I wanted to have a whole pot of money of my own some day; maybe not as much as the Roosevelts, but lots of dough. It's just that I didn't want the government to help me get it. Of course, I wanted big, powerful cars, too, but not the chauffeur-driven kind the Roosevelts rode around in. I wondered what happened to old FDR's collection of Packards after he died. It would be something to own one of those. Forget it. My aging Ford needed transmission work and I didn't know how I would pay for that.

I was a young man with ambition and an attitude. At the hotel where she greeted Huron's movers and shakers, questions were invited. I had the audacity to question her husband's handling of our entry into World War II as well as his reasoning behind the New Deal welfare state.

I was, in actual fact, a smart assed news reporter totally out of line. Eleanor's

answers were courteous – more courteous than I deserved – and they were condescending. She managed to ignore me during the rest of the question-and-answer part of her whirlwind appearance. I learned from that experience, but it was decades later before I realized that I was experiencing, first hand, a sad stage in the metamorphosis of America.

Get where you wanted to be before dark

The country's liberalization, for which Eleanor and her husband had campaigned so vigorously, was only in its infancy. The culture that would give birth to the thought-and-motion-control police was still in the future.

Even Eleanor – bless her soul – could not have envisioned the totality of her movement's success. Intimate, erotic, one-on-one driving relations with one's car would brand you an environmental outcast. Lone drivers daring to intrude upon special "ride share" routes – "Frenzalong" Freeways – would be promptly arrested.

People actually drove cars at speeds well in excess of 55 miles and hour – legally! It was a glorious time for the expression of independent thought and action. If you are now under age 50, you missed it; you have already lived most of your life shackled with ever-tightening government control; and you have no concept of what it would be like to drive fast without fear of imminent arrest.

Let me tell you about it. Just after my meeting with Eleanor, I hopped into my hopped-up '49 Ford "newscruiser" and headed for South Dakota's "West River" country. Speed limits were then 70, as I recall, but the important thing was that nobody got all uptight about speed limits. People were actually permitted some slack to use their own good judgment. Out on the lonely, open stretches of South Dakota, you just naturally mashed the gas pedal a little. It felt good. Free. Soul satisfying. Besides, it was the only way to get from point A to point B in time for supper; or back to the newsroom with a hot story, complete with pictures.

My "beat" for the *Daily Plainsman,* The Associated Press, The United Press and, later, for magazines, covered the Dakotas, Montana, Minnesota, Iowa and Wisconsin. The operative word was "covered". It was possible – and permissible – to cover ground and gobble up road. I went through a good many "previously owned" cars in those largely government-free days. Some, I remember with particular fondness.

There was the hulking Lincoln Zephyr, vintage 1939, that was pure joy on the open road and pure hell at refueling time. This was followed by a sleek, black '48 Caddy, an orange-red '54 Studebaker Starliner and more. From first hand, arrest-free experience, I knew the top speed and performance limitations of each of them.

Montana had speed limits, but only after dark. The trick, of course, was to get where you wanted to be before dark. Nevada and even staid old Iowa had no limits except "safe and reasonable". There was life before government control, and it was good. To me it was "free range" living. I wanted it to go on forever. And I had a plan to make it happen.

Eleanor, if you are looking down on all this; I know you and Franklin meant well, but things are sorta' getting out of hand.

■ ■ ■

DRIVE CARS YOU CAN'T HAVE AT SPEEDS YOU WOULDN'T DARE; EXPLORE, FANTASIZE, LEARN

Let the "main stream" media fret about their loss of liberal power. Auto journalists – far more competent at their craft – will introduce you to real power: piston power. Ride with them as they take on Italy's mountain switchbacks in the reborn, 500-horsepower supercar, the Bugatti EB110. Project yourself into the fantasy: you are at the wheel and you are one helluva fearless, foot-heavy driver. Not every editor liked the car, but it was one erotic experience as far as you were concerned.

Now back to a more attainable dream. You've decided that a macho guy like yourself needs a sports utility vehicle (SUV). But which one? Your favorite auto journalists can help you decide. With pictures and precise detail, they will take you along on comprehensive and crushingly brutal test drives of every SUV available. They'll go places and do things to these SUV"s that you could probably never do. Then they'll give you the pro's and con's with some strong personal opinions thrown in.

Give your auto addiction a regular dose of adrenaline; pick up your favorite car magazine; hours of dreaming, exploring and learning. You can even sign on as a real life driver for some of their adventures.

Frenzalong

The Frenzalong Cargoyle grunts with glee whenever he sees a car filled with people. ■ "Stuff 'em in! Stuff 'em in!" he chortles with unabashed joy. ■ In dark, dank underground laboratories, Eco-Freaks programmed Frenzalong to lead the "ride share" campaign; stuff every car everywhere in the world, yours included. ■ "Lone drivers destroy our planet," the Eco-Freaks yelled after Frenzalong as he stumbled and groped his way out of their labs. His mission, they knew, would never lack for money. Frenzalong Freeways sprouted up in cities everywhere; lonely, empty expanses of concrete reserved exclusively for caring folks with full cars. Wasteful social engineering with your money? Not as Frenzalong fans see it. Even as you read this, they are concocting new laws to – get this – punish your boss if you dare drive alone to work. Think what that will do for your career.

■ ■ ■

You drive alone.
Could this be wrong?
Beware of meeting
Frenzalong.

He'll stuff your car
with friends and neighbors.
"It'll save the earth
these noble labors!"

CHAPTER 14

"FREE RANGE" FOREVER;
ROADS TO RICHES

It was late spring, 1954. I was piloting my twin pipe Ford, vintage '49, through South Dakota's sprawling "West River" cattle country, coming home with a good story and pictures, when it hit me.

Do this for life?

"Damn, this is fun! What if I could just keep on doing this for the rest of my life? Cruising the back roads. Thousands of wonderful miles of backroads. Exploring for stories. Meeting and enjoying the people involved in those stories."

I was enthralled with the process of getting to and from my work over roads that climbed, swooped down along creek beds, twisted, turned and sometimes opened up to pedal-to-the-metal straightaways. Heaven for an AED addicted farm boy. Even before my AED syndrome became undeniable, country roads and roadsides got into my soul. You only get the feel for it walking barefoot, preferably with a dog at your side. Country roads have rickety, narrow bridges that span streams full of childhood adventure: turtles, crayfish, bullheads and lots of cool water for your feet. Country roads have ditches where pheasants hide, gophers run and, except for the bird songs, they have wonderful silence.

Later in life, I would be privileged to drive John Denver around in one of my "special interest" cars. He sang almost the whole while. As I listened to him sing his hit song "Country Roads", I was thrilled but still wondered if he really loved country roads as I did.

Some people think while driving; I think out loud. Helps to really sort things out. Especially when you are alone at the wheel and not another human in sight. Especially when you are thinking through a big idea.

"So you want to do this backroads thing for the rest of your life. What's the big idea about that? Just tell your *Plainsman* bosses you love your job and you want to sign up for life. Well, just a damn minute. There's a catch. I want to make unlimited bushels of money; more money than the *Plainsman* would ever think of paying me. I want to have my own company. Pick my own stories. Set my own deadlines. Be my own boss. Okay, that would be a big idea, Kenneth old boy, if you could pull it off."

My "what if" thinking aloud was interrupted by the reality that my faithful Ford was about to run out of gas. This was not a territory where I wanted to walk to the nearest gas station or, worse, sleep in the car till help arrived. I was in luck, just around the bend was a little town; more a wide spot in the road but with a sign that said "gas". A grizzled but smiling old guy greeted me with a "howdy", then proceeded to pump gas; not in my car but in the cylindrical glass enclosure that wrapped the antiquated round pump. When full, the calibrations on the glass measured the gas going into my tank.

I chat about the weather, the crops, about anything just to prolong the enjoyment of this journey back home and back into time. The proprietor looks as old as his gas pump. Undoubtedly, he has decided long ago that his business volume didn't justify any new fangled pumping equipment. His dog, sleeping in the doorway of the ramshackle station, looked to be pushing 80 in dog years. Back of the station some 25 feet or more is his house. It appears to be kept up by a wife more concerned with beauty and order than the station operator. The house needs paint but looks neat as a pin with frilly curtains at the windows and geraniums flourishing along the foundation.

Author Ken with the fabled "Newscruiser" – a 1949 Ford "updated" with pseudo 1951 Crestliner trim.

I pay for my gas and am on my way; but not before thinking, "I'll bet there's a story here. How did they meet? How long have they been married? What happened in their lives before they settled in here?"

BOND WITH PEOPLE WHO KNOW WHAT IT MEANS TO REALLY LOVE THEIR CARS

They are happily addicted and I am proud to be one of them. We may be a vanishing breed; but we're too busy having fun to worry about it. You can join us. Pick a car club of your choice; pay dues that will probably be less than fifty bucks including the club magazine. Why, you can even join the Ferrari Club and not own a Ferrari.

Car people – with a few unfortunate exceptions – are just plain nice folks. The primary purpose of every club is to help you have more fun with your car. We don't do protest marches. We don't seek victimhood status. The most explosive device we handle is an overheated brat on the grill. We look out for each other. If that old classic of yours breaks down on some remote rally road, other members will come and rescue you. Not incidentally, you will see some of the world's most beautiful countryside on auto rallies; all the while you are sharpening your skills at maneuvering tricky roads. Skill, not speed, determines the winner. Not infrequently, the proceeds from rally fees go to charity.

Get involved in auto crossing, gymkhanas or out and out racing if you prefer. Enter concours events to show off your impeccably groomed chariot. Attend national events wherein getting there is at least half the fun. Being there and making new friends is the other half. Most clubs sponsor international events, too; maybe one that includes picking up that new car direct from the factory.

It's us against a world overrun by the auto immune. Join now.

Finding compelling stories where none seemed to exist was a self taught ability honed by necessity at the *Daily Plainsman*. I had two basic choices. I could report back to the newsroom that "nothing is happening", which was usually the case in Huron and the surrounding counties. Making this choice meant that the national news wires would dominate each day's editions; and I would be bored out of my skull. Maybe out of a job too. My second basic course of action – the one I opted for without hesitation – was to "create" news. It was a matter of finding and fertilizing the germ of a story somewhere, anywhere. I learned to look beyond and beneath the obvious. Mostly, it was a matter of developing a sixth sense for stories that were going on all around me.

"Damn it! I'm pretty good at this work." I was thinking aloud again. The gauche green Ford was wound up and headed for Huron. "My stories are making the national wires. I'm getting good response from my column. This is not a one-time-one-place career path. It's a capability. I should be able to get more money for it. But keep the fun."

My mind kept coming back to all the little weekly newspapers that dotted the countryside. *The Bugle, The Herald, The Sentinel, The Reporter, The Gazette, The News* and on an on. Each had its routine: selling ads, gathering "news" of local happenings like marriages, births, deaths, church suppers and whatever else could possibly contribute to still another week's edition.

"What about buying a weekly column from Ken Kamstra? Interesting, colorful human interest stuff that will add sparkle – and fill space – in every edition from now till forever?"

That was it! The key ingredients to my big idea: a product and a market to buy the product. I would promise an exciting new column every week; exclusive, no reprints of old stuff. Stories like how Pony Express riders look back on their careers; who won the battle for Sitting Bull's remains; what farmers really think of state-sponsored irrigation and more.

My idea-generating gears were churning as fast as those propelling my Ford. Before I realized it, I was pulling into one of my favorite parking-ruminating spots on a bluff overlooking the Missouri River and Pierre, the South Dakota capital. Just across the river, I had camped with a Smithsonian Institute crew as they excavated thousand-year-old Arikara Indian villages. Theirs was an urgent mission to finish before the giant Oahe Dam would flood these villages, hiding history's secrets into eternity.

Creating these stories brought a valuable, humbling perspective; my own insignificance in the relentless march of time. A sense of forever. I wondered if the meadowlarks singing around me now would be singing on this hilltop thousands of years after my departure. Probably.

Then, in a crass return to entrepreneurial motivation, I wondered how weekly news editors would respond to some new stories on the saga of the disappearing Arikara tribes. Stories written just for them.

I made my decision to go for it! First, draft a letter to all of South Dakota's weekly newspaper editors. It would be filled with inarguable logic and an offer they couldn't refuse. For just $8 per week, they would get a great "Prairie Rambler" column from me. They could even ask me to do special assignments. As a clincher, I would include a recommendation from the head of the Weekly Newspaper Editors Association.

Pure entrepreneurial genius

Maybe it wasn't such a great idea

Auto Immunes who prefer guiding shiftless, sound-deadened, automated marshmallows over mind numbing freeways, could never comprehend my enthusiasm for this emerging concept. People who love roads that challenge themselves and their cars would not only understand but be more than a little jealous. If it worked.

It would be pure entrepreneurial genius.

"I don't want our baby to have an unemployed father," was the sobering observation of my beautiful and very pregnant wife.

This – life would eventually teach us – is the crucial test for every aspiring entrepreneur and the answer is not always obvious. The risk is. Invariably, an entrepreneurial venture demands surrender of the comfortable and the secure for a venture that might work. Or might not.

Sometimes the idea is lousy or at least needs more work. Sometimes the timing isn't right. I decided on the middle ground: eliminate most of the risk by getting paid subscribers up front. If it worked, maybe the new baby could have a nursery room of her own. We loved our one-bedroom apartment, but Mom and Dad and two kids in one bedroom could get a bit crowded.

We talked into the night; a debate we would have many more times in our lives. No matter how well things were going, I would always have bigger dreams. Tomorrow, I would launch the direct mail campaign of my life!

The letters went out. We waited. Responses – with checks – dribbled in: 10%, 15%. 20%. 30% and finally 32%. One weekly editor even offered to hire me part time until the idea got going. Then the letters stopped coming in.

I was devastated. What went wrong? Almost two thirds of the editors ignored my offer. As a practicing ad guy years later, I realized that a 32% response should have been a cause for celebration. It was absolutely crushing to me then. I was crushed; I suspect wife, Mimi, was secretly relieved.

"She was right," I thought, "maybe it wasn't such a great idea after all."

That night, after five year old daughter, Linda, was tucked in bed, Mimi and I sat at the kitchen table. We had worked at this same table stuffing envelopes only three weeks ago and now we were doing it again. This time, painfully, we were returning checks to those editors and publishers who had responded.

"At least I still have a job," I said to Mimi, knowing she would take comfort in that fact in view of her ever enlarging belly. With that, I was out the door and off to the post office. It wasn't easy to let go of an idea and it hurt even more to give back money when we needed every dollar we could get.

Just as I was rushing upstairs on the return to our apartment, the phone rang. It was Bruce Campbell, my boss.

"Ken?"

"Yes."

"This is Bruce. Bob Lusk just got back from a publishers convention. He's heard something about you trying to start your own publishing company or something. I told him I didn't know anything about it, but he wants to see you first thing in the morning."

"My God!" It was all I could stammer. I babbled something about it all being a mistake after agreeing to meet Lusk. He was both owner and publisher of the *Plainsman*. As such, he didn't usually show up at the office "first thing", which worried me even more.

Mimi had probably never seen me so shaken. She looked so serene, sitting there so "heavy with child" that I couldn't tell her I was about to be fired. She was looking at a guy who had just failed at entrepreneurism and now was about to be unemployed as well. I made up a yarn about Bruce wanting to go over a feature with me and turned in early. I didn't sleep much. Why in hell didn't I keep those checks until tomorrow morning! At least I would have a business venture if not a job.

Entrepreneurs need a large amount of patience

Next morning, I dressed more neatly than usual, but not with tie. Only Mr. Lusk wore ties at the *Plainsman*. I arrived at the *Plainsman* before eight and went directly to his paneled office on the first floor. Only Mr. Lusk had a real office with a door, a leather couch and a look of success. I wanted an office like his someday. I didn't want to spend much time in such an office, I just fantasized about having an important looking office and a fat salary to go with it.

"Fat chance!" I almost said aloud as I entered Lusk's office. He always seemed to be a kindly man. Tall, silver haired. Distinguished. He looked exactly like the publisher of one of the state's foremost newspapers should look.

Right now, he only looked stern.

"Ken's what's all this about your wanting to sell stories to weekly newspapers?" he asked and then, before I could answer, pulled one of my "sample" columns from his desk. "Is this yours?"

He was moving in for the kill. I was about to be the unemployed father.

"Yes," I said and then explained how I thought it would be a great new advance for South Dakota journalism. I told him how much I enjoyed doing feature stories. I was rambling and I knew it.

"You've got a good career right here. Someday you will be an executive editor or even a publisher. But I don't think you are quite ready yet.

Then he gave me a raise. Starting immediately, I would be earning $75 a week; a full $5 a week more.

"Thank you, Mr. Lusk," I said trying to play it cool and not show the immense flood of relief I felt at still having a job much less a raise. I wanted to say something more but couldn't. I turned to leave.

" By the way, I liked your stories about the Arikara villages, " Lusk said as I was making my exit.

"I didn't get fired! I still had a job!" I wanted to shout it all over the *Plainsman* as I met the staff coming in for work. Instead, I just wore a smug smile knowing I would soon have an extra $20 a month for the family budget.

I happily returned to my beat, but the "Free Range Living" concept stuck somewhere in the back of my mind. Angela, our new daughter, was welcomed as the fourth occupant of our single bedroom.

By July of the following year, I would be uprooting my newly enlarged family, this time for another journalist's job. Davidson Publishing Company, Duluth, Minnesota. Business magazines. For now, I would content myself with being an employee, a follower of someone else's dream. The entrepreneurial flame inside me hadn't gone out; I would just bank the fires and bide my time.

Being an entrepreneur takes guts. Mine just weren't toughened up enough yet. Entrepreneurs also need a large measure of impatience. Impatient people seize opportunities, drive dreams, make ideas come alive. Meanwhile, the Ken Kamstra family moved into our first real, rented, house with two bedrooms. No garage but a continuing opportunity to take on backroads. On company time.

■ ■ ■

New daughter, new job; idea on hold

CHAPTER 15   A SUITE AT THE WALDORF

A nation of movie-goers laughed when "Crocodile Dundee", in scruffy leather jacket and attitude to match, descended on New York City direct from the outback's and hinterlands of Australia. Only a few snooty bell hops laughed when I descended on New York's Waldorf Astoria. It was 1955 and I, too, was scruffy, leather jacketed and direct from the hinterlands of Duluth, Minnesota, home of my new job.

"I stood there amidst the grandeur and the glitter of the Waldorf Astoria's lobby. I was transfixed, awe struck, dumb founded. New York City! The famous Waldorf Astoria! This was not a typical day on the job by any stretch of the imagination. It was evidence, I rationalized, of the wisdom of broadening my work horizons beyond the Dakotas.

"Kenny, you're not in South Dakota anymore," I chuckled, at the same time vowing not to be intimidated by these city slickers and all their ostentation. Still, I wished I had at least polished my shoes and maybe pressed my pants. Too late now. Hell, I already was intimidated if I really wanted to level with myself. This is a hotel known the world over for catering to the rich and famous. My early life as U. S. Navy and Merchant Marine sailor, had brought me to many a seaport honky tonk and even New York, but never anywhere near the Waldorf Astoria.

"What am I doing here?"

It was time to make my move. Any moment, I expected all the hustle and bustle in the lobby to come to a sudden stop. At that moment, everyone would turn to this unworthy interloper in their midst and in one voice they would challenge me.

"Yessss?"

Would that I could be back behind the wheel searching out stories in Minnesota and Wisconsin; soothing my ever-present AED urges. I couldn't. I had to take the initiative. Assuming my most purposeful stride, head held high, I marched forward to the massively ornate reservations counter. It was a kind of kingdom within a kingdom.

"I believe you have a room reserved for Kamstra, Ken Kamstra," I announced, striving for an air of nonchalance, even bored disdain for the plebeian, tedious details of travel.

"Waldo Waldorf" was neither deceived nor impressed. Incredulous maybe, but not the least impressed. His haughtiness, in fact, seemed to intensify with each additional minute of our encounter. He glared first at me and then at my left elbow. I was leaning on his marble topped counter. Instantly, I removed the offending appendage from his counter and with it all further pretense that checking into hotels like the Waldorf was routine for me.

Good Lord, I was almost standing at attention; it was World War II all over again and I was the new recruit. Finally, Waldo spoke.

"And how are we spelling that?" he asked with a tone of condescension that added an unspoken, "you insufferable peasant! "

Without question and with little effort on his part, Waldo had definitely gained the upper hand. I spelled my name for him, feeling like a kid in a fourth grade spelling bee. He offered no further acknowledgment. Waldo turned away to consult his registration records. He returned, obviously crestfallen at actually finding my name among the reserved guests.

"Ah yes, Mr. Cawm-straw, here it is. "

His pronunciation of '"Cawm-straw" apparently gave the name a sophisticated ring, perhaps more befitting a guest of the prestigious Waldorf Astoria. The entire episode must have been unnerving, not to mention repugnant, to a man

"You insufferable peasant!"

of his stature. Worse, due to a scheduling foul up, he had to put me up in one of the lavish tower suites until my room became available next day.

Bell hops made no effort to assist me with my tacky suitcases as I made my way to the elevators. I probably didn't look like a guest to them. Maybe a maintenance man of some kind. Certainly not a tipper.

They were right about the tipping. I knew to the penny how much money there was in the family bank account back home and it didn't leave room for any high living, Waldorf or no. Nonetheless it had been a long flight, a harrowing cab ride and an even more taxing encounter with Waldo. I had definitely earned a drink.

"Room service? Please send up a pint of bourbon and some ice."

I tipped the boy fifty cents. His dismay was exceeded only by his disbelief as he gazed around my spacious suite. Marble bathrooms – each one bigger than our kitchen at home – anchored either end. A bed obviously intended for group sex occupied center stage and was flanked by ornate writing desks. Below my throne room was Central Park and New York City in all its glory. Not a car lovers' town, not a place for "Free Range" living, but something to experience.

"Everyone should spend at least one night of his life in a suite at the Waldorf," I said as I poured a generous bourbon over ice. "and as for you, Waldo, go suck a lemon! "

I really felt no bitterness toward Waldo and the people who could afford to live like this. These surroundings only intensified my desire to excel. Liberal Socialists, I knew, would advocate stripping the wealth from every Waldorf Astoria guest and then turning the hotel into digs for the down and out. I wanted to join the affluent; they wanted to destroy them. At this stage of my life, I really didn't think about class struggles, however, I only thought about my own struggles to succeed.

As the bourbon warmed my belly and my brain, I looked out over the expanse of lights that was New York after dark. Bourbon always helped me put things into perspective. Life was truly an exciting, infinite adventure. I couldn't wait for each new chapter to unfold.

Tomorrow was reality time. My job was to interview conventioning paper industry execs; fodder for one of my bosses trade magazines, *Paper Sales*. Publishing a daily newspaper at this event was not the essence of journalistic success, I knew, but it was career progress.

The bourbon helped, I knew, but I was even beginning to see Waldo in a more charitable light. There was, after all, more than just the 2,000 miles of "fly over country" separating his world from mine. He couldn't be happy in my open country world; nor could I tolerate New York living. Without question, Waldo was among the Auto Immune majority in an Auto Immune city.

Anyway, here I was in New York City, all expenses paid by my new bosses at Davidson Publishing Company. Company headquarters were in Duluth; sales offices in New York.

■ ■ ■

Marshall Reinig, a gruff, no nonsense entrepreneur, was the driving force behind the modest sized Davidson Publishing Company empire. He had moved his company headquarters from Chicago to Duluth ostensibly for health reasons. Whatever the reasons, his publishing enterprise continued to flourish.

Life was truly an exciting, infinite adventure

His growing success was evidence to me that a driver can drive his dream from almost anywhere he chooses to be.

Reinig chose Duluth where he not only reestablished his publishing company but simultaneously went into business raising mink on a mink ranch he purchased north of the city. The ranch – clinging to the Lake Superior shore line – was typical of his shrewd money making genius. Among the many trade magazines in the Davidson Publishing stable was the *American Fur Breeder.* This respected authority on domestic fur breeding mixed industry news with "how to" success stories for mink ranchers.

Steppin' up. The 1948 Series 62 Cadillac four door sedan.

Not a few of these stories were written by Ken Kamstra. I reached these story assignments behind the wheel of my latest auto acquisition: a silky smooth '48 Caddy, lovingly owned previously by a Duluth matron. I do believe the Caddy had more fun with me than her. Getting to the stories was fun, mink ranching interviews were not. There is a stench about a mink ranch no matter how amiable its operator. Mink coats may look smooth and sexy draped over the female body but, on the hoof, minks are smelly creatures and mean as hell. They would as soon bite your finger off as look at you.

Reinig's ranching venture simultaneously provided him with first hand knowledge for his magazine plus a healthy cash flow from the sale of mink pelts. The nitwit Animal Rights Movement had not yet come to power, probably because prospective members would have found little time for such asinine "causes" as they struggled to earn a living. The Liberal Socialists take over of America was still in its infancy and as yet unable to fund such random idiocy. And so it was that entrepreneurs like Reinig could raise mink without fear of punishment for violating "mink rights". Women, who could afford to indulge

I poured a second bourbon to toast my upward mobility, albeit not as far upward as my marble-silk-and-walnut suite would suggest. I wondered what guys like Waldo do when they go home each night. Would he enjoy the same power when interacting with his wife and kids? Or, like me, would he eat tuna hot dishes to make ends meet. Oh well.

Poor Waldo didn't know what else Davidson had in store for him. I was only the advance man for the Davidson crew to follow. More indignities were due for the venerable Waldorf. My task was to establish a working schedule and system with our New York printer. Photos, art, ads and copy had to be at the printer by midnight daily. It was my job to coordinate, to make page layout decisions, to get everything right. This was before computers, "Spell Check" and all that. It was purely people skills.

It was just after 2 a.m. on the final day of our four-day ordeal when the cabby dropped me off at the Waldorf. This day's issue was "put to bed" in the jargon of the publishing business. I was more than anxious to put myself to bed as well. My mind and body were drained from 19 hours of continuous, hectic effort.

The night was refreshingly crisp. September air filled my lungs, washing away the heat and replacing the stench of the press rooms. In my hotel room, no longer a suite, I fought off exhaustion long enough to gaze out at the moonlit city. My thoughts turned to those eerie nights in the Arikara Indian villages of South Dakota. This same, eons-old moon illuminated men and women whose lifetimes had been lived out thousands of years before New York City was ever conceived.

The forever perspective again. I revisited it often at night. It was becoming a ritual with me: strive for maximum performance by day; rekindle dreams in the tranquillity of night.

"Where will I be, what will I have done with my life when this moon looks down on me ten years from now, twenty years from now?"

> *More indignities were due*

"Ken, you bazzard…"

I didn't ponder long. Seconds after my head hit the down-filled pillow, I was lost in deep sleep.

Suddenly, there was a thunderous pounding on my door. I tried to ignore it and cling to my precious sleep. The pounding only got louder.

"Ken, you bazzard, I know yer in ere! Ken, get up! We got prob…problems!'

The sonofabitch was drunk. I would know that voice anywhere. It was Jim, the photographer. We always hired him for these out of town gigs. Drunk was not unusual for him or for most photographers I knew for that matter. But what the hell was he doing pounding on my door?

"Just a damn minute!" I yelled, rolling out of bed and into my trousers in one awkward motion. I stumbled to the door and opened it. The light spilled in from the hallway and onto my wrist watch.

"For Christ's sake, Jim, it's three in the morning. Why don't you sleep it off and whatever the problem is we'll talk about it in the morning…"

"Ken, you ash hole, we got…we got problems. You gotta help me. Now!"

I had seen Jim drunk before but never like this. His face was ashen. There was sheer terror in his eyes.

"Okay, Jim," I said, "lets go look at this problem if its so damned important. But I'm telling you, I gotta get some sleep, you dumb shit!"

Actually, I liked Jim. He was a good photographer and generally reliable with or without booze. Right now, though, it was hard to be chummy with the guy. Jim staggered down the hallway and I paddled along behind him, bare feet, bare chest and barely awake. His room was just down the hall and around the corner. It was the nerve center of our make shift publishing operation. The "photo lab", we called it. Window blinds were taped shut to create dark room conditions. Chemical bottles were everywhere intermixed with expended whiskey bottles, beer bottles, cigarette butts and junk. Overhead, wires were strung to hold negatives yet to be printed. The elegant bath tub had been pressed into service for rinsing chemicals during the print-making process. Water in the filled tub overflowed into the overflow drain, taking the excess chemicals with it. All in all, it was an ingenious conversion of an otherwise limited use hotel room.

Since the bathtub had been commandeered for photo lab services, I could only assume that Jim had suspended bathing for the duration. Today at noon, the big convention would come to an end and so would our Waldorf operation. I looked forward to a good night's sleep at home.

Jim's room was just ahead. As we approached his door, I was shocked into a fully awakened state by cold water oozing around my bare feet. The lush hallway carpet – God knows what the Waldorf paid for this stuff –was saturated with foul-smelling water.

"What in hell is happening here?" I was fully awake by now..

"Jush hole your damn horses and you'll see."

Jim still looked terrified in spite of his bluster. His breath stank of sour whiskey and nicotine.

Jim fumbled with his key in the door for what seemed an eternity. Finally, it opened. I didn't want to believe my eyes. Water was standing inches deep everywhere in the room. Photo prints, scrap paper and other debris floated atop the

Reinig got the news and the bill

water. As we stepped into the room, our footsteps caused still more water to slosh out into the hallway.

"I juss fell asleep. Plain crapped out. Unnerstand whut I'm tellin' you, Kenneth?" He knew I hated the name "Kenneth". It was a name I always heard just before some big kid at school put his fist in my scrawny face. It was Jim's way of fighting back, trying to regain some self esteem. Jim was babbling. He tried to flop back onto his bed. Maybe he thought it was all a bad dream, that when he woke up again it would be gone.

I kept him awake and kept him talking. In spite of his incoherence, it was relatively easy to piece together what happened. While Jim slept, photo prints sucked into the bathtub overflow drain. The water – constantly running as part of the photo finishing process – simply cascaded over the rim of the tub and out into the carpeted room.

"You dumb bastard!" It was as sympathetic as I could be just then.

Waldo would tell his superiors that he was right all along about that scurvy gang from Duluth, Minnesota.

Marshall Reinig's expletives would surely be heard all the way to Duluth. This particular publishing venture was not going to be very profitable for him. The Waldorf's bill for damages would have to cover recarpeting one room, one section of hallway plus "miscellaneous materials and labor". Then, of course, there would be the matter of lost room rental until it could finally be readied for guests again. And, oh yes, the same would be true for the room just below; plus a new ceiling and fixtures.

I arranged to be across town making final arrangements with the printers when Reinig got the news and the bill.

■ ■ ■

Life and my career moved on. There would be other on site publishing activities in Chicago and elsewhere. I would spend a great deal of time driving, flying, criss crossing America doing stories to sustain the editorial content of the many Davidson publications. In the process – since this was the core of almost every story – I was learning how and why business leaders excel. Not exactly my "Prairie Rambler" concept, but no office confinement either.

Life and career moved on

Meanwhile, Mimi would be home in Duluth, caring for our demanding young daughters and an even more demanding coal-fired furnace. Nonetheless, she loved having a whole house to herself, friendly neighbors, and a beautiful – if sometimes brutal – city.

When you're enjoying your work, when your boss likes the way you work, when your family is happily settled in and feeling secure, why in hell would you want to leave? That's what an exasperated Marshall Reinig wanted to know when I walked in and quit. For the second time in my journalistic career, I was getting the "two year itch". Mostly it was instinctive, an urge to move on. Always, I was aware that two wars and not a little personal indecision had given me a late start on the success ladder.

"My God," I thought, "I'm already thirty years old." Being thirty was the beginning of "over the hill" as I saw it. I wrote a piece on "facing man's mortality". It was heavy stuff for a thirty year old and intellectually over my head. Still, it seemed to help me refocus my career compass.

"Do you want more money? A bigger office? What is it?"

"Lady Marion". While hubby chases down stories in his big black '48 Caddy, Marion – known as "Mimi" to those lucky enough to be close to her – holds down the home fort.

Reinig didn't, probably couldn't understand. My destiny was waiting. It was a higher destiny than any "good job" could fulfill. Reinig, in fact, had contributed to my vision of the future. I had come to really like the guy. On business trips to Chicago, for instance, we would go for long walks through his old neighborhood. He owned businesses, he owned buildings, he owned land. I could sense the immense satisfaction in his voice as we retraced his youthful haunts and the birthplace of his entrepreneurial rise.

> *"Why not go into advertising?"*

I, too, wanted to know that satisfaction. Duluth wouldn't do. In Duluth, there was only one other writing job and that was the daily newspaper. I saw that as a move downward or sideways at best.

The author trying hard to look the part of "sophisticated" magazine journalist.

My dilemma, experienced even more painfully by Mimi and daughters was deja vu Huron. There, too, my bosses offered me inducements to stay on. There, too, I liked my job, my coworkers workers and my life. Nonetheless I was learning a basic truth: success and "settling in" too soon in the game are often diametrically opposed. Magazine journalism had advanced my horizons literally and figuratively. Still…

"Why not go into advertising?"

Mimi had a way of getting right to the nub of things without all the philosophical BS I was prone to include. It was a radical idea. Heresy. Journalism, for all its meager pay and lousy hours, was, I thought, the purest expression of the writer's art. Advertising, I suspected, was a world populated by hucksters and charlatans.

It was an idea that generated no little amount of soul searching. I wasn't sure whether Mimi advanced the concept out of confidence in my creativity or out of concern for our budget-dominated life style.

"Hell, let's do it," I said in the second night of our deliberation.

This time, though, it had to be different. We would concentrate on the "Twin Cities" of Minneapolis and St. Paul. In this metropolitan area, there would be literally hundreds of options. No more nomadic moves from town to town to accommodate my job changes. Or maybe other enterprises.

Scores of resumés, follow up calls and face to face interviews followed. To my chagrin, Twin Cities ad agencies were unimpressed with my credentials.

"One day, they might wish they'd hired me when I'd come cheap." I said.

I did find a job in a corporate ad department; and I came cheap. Time to call the movers again. We hated Duluth when we arrived. Now there would be sadness at leaving; a sadness amplified by Lake Superior fog horns. There is no sound on earth more incessantly saddening than the "ooawmph ooawmph" of fog horns. During our first night in Duluth, we were both a bit depressed and homesick as we listened to them all night long. Now we would miss them.

Shunned by ad agencies, I would be reporting to the ad department of a large international corporation.

Ad agencies unimpressed with Kamstra credentials

■ ■ ■

CHAPTER 16

HOW THE "GOLDEN OX" BECAME THE GOLDEN GOOSE

"Creative genius"

More than 300 guys gathered in the famous Sun Valley ski resort in Idaho that weekend. The feminist movement hadn't been invented yet. This was a horny, hard driving, all male sales force participating in an annual ritual known as the national sales meeting.

The mood was jovial. Men, some young and trim, many aging and bulging from too much expense account living, renewed old acquaintances and made new ones. Conversations focused on shop talk heavily laced with boisterous recounting of the past night's fortunes at card games or games of chance in the local bistros. Their quarry – more often fantasy than reality – was the comely and generously endowed "snow bunnies" who worked at the sprawling resort in exchange for meager pay, tips and skiing privileges. Some, the more naive, also held out hope of meeting their Prince Charming. Mingling with this group, the bunnies would find themselves mostly kissing frogs.

That was their problem. Mine was to see that the entire three day event – so carefully orchestrated weeks in advance – would be flawlessly executed. Some day, I thought, it would be nice to be an invited guest participant at one of these affairs; feted, fed, wined, entertained, schmoozed, presented to, lectured to and, above all, motivated. If management's spare-no-expense investment was to pay off, every man would return to his sales territory a new man, recharged and ready to kill the enemy.

It would be nice to be the recipient of such attention. Still in all, it was not bad to be the "creative genius" behind this extravaganza. The creative process began for me well before the meeting. I was then a few months into "doing my own thing", enroute to Atlanta.

"Will this be your first visit to Atlanta? "

The nice little old lady sitting next to me on the plane was trying to make conversation. But I had serious thinking to do.

"Yes it is," I replied, making no effort to extend the conversation and, instead, peering officiously into my brief case. I liked little old ladies, often made an effort to learn from old people. Their wisdom added perspective to my life. Right now, I wanted to think deeply about that life; I didn't want to visit.

I took out my new business cards again and admired them. "Kamstra Communications, Inc." Beautiful. Professionally designed, three-color. Someone once told me there was a law of inverse proportion about business cards: "the smaller the company the more ornate the business card." Certainly, I confirmed this law. Big corporations, like my client picking up the tab for this Atlanta junket, could settle for discreet, one-color cards. I needed to make a statement; they had already made theirs by virtue of being world wide and world famous. My statement was the high design card and copy line – italics, screened 50% – that read, "it takes more than ads to move people."

"It takes more than ads to move people". That line, defined as "positioning" by the experts that abound in the ad business, was more than that; it was my absolute commitment. Admittedly by sheer dumb luck much of the time, I had been preparing much of my adult life to now claim expertise in "moving people." Journalism was at the core of it. Good communications – whether to move people or products – began with journalistic skills to find the story or find the direction. I wanted to move the people who move the products. If I could help clients motivate and "move" their people, their companies would most assuredly prosper. And so would I. My "preparation" for creating my own company began with newspaper journalism, followed by magazine journalism. To think I got paid, albeit meagerly, for analyzing the people and the strategies behind successful companies.

A cynical writer friend of mine, describing corporate mission statements, said, "they're like finding a bullet hole in the wall, then painting a target around it with the bullet hole in dead center".

This could have been said about my zig zag career path. In retrospect, it all seemed to have been part of a mission, a plan and a purpose. In truth, I only knew I wanted to keep "thinking higher", moving up and moving on. In the process, I added direct selling, big corporation advertising/sales promotion experience plus a stint with an employee communications firm. I worked with Larry Wilson, a super salesman who in turn led me to a job with the late

"Kamstra Communications, Inc."

billionaire super salesman, Curt Carlson. Invaluable experience. Larry built a worldwide firm teaching others how to sell. Curt built a multi-billion dollar empire encompassing hotels, restaurants, travel and more. I like to think I helped a little; mostly I learned.

"It takes more than ads to move people"

Now – "late in life" at 35 – it was time for me to try my wings and fly solo. Hell, even my warship and oreboat experience brought "real life" experience to my credentials.

"It takes more than ads to move people". I had earned the right to say that. To believe that.

Media reps of the nation not to worry. Kamstra Communications was only Ken Kamstra – with bookkeeping help from wife Mimi – working unobtrusively in the corner of his basement. Sharing space with the laundry room.

Author's "almost" sports car, a 1954 Studebaker. Sleek, tomato red, fast (kinda').

"If we ever write a book about all this," I said to Mimi, " it should be entitled "Never On Mondays". Mondays, of course, were laundry days; not good days to invite clients out to visit my fledgling agency. She didn't seem to appreciate the humor of it . I had, after all, once again left a significant and secure "big corporation" job for the challenge of operating my own agency.

My kidding about the book was, in fact, false bravado. Truth was, I was scared. Scared as hell. Why would anyone in his right mind give up a successful executive career – with regular paychecks, profit sharing, perks and all – to start over as a loner working out of his basement?

Think higher

Think higher. Beware of getting too comfortable with where you are and what you are. It was a merciless, task master philosophy. Years later, I would produce a motivational film, "Think Higher", that would be modestly successful, but that's getting ahead of the story.

Living out this philosophy wasn't easy for Mimi. But she was a brave trooper. In advanced pregnancy, she had even hitch hiked with me enroute to one of my many "new jobs." In time, each new job began to improve our bank account, but that didn't make all the pain go away.

One of my first accounts after discarding the corporate security blanket was a company that manufactured toilet seats. Few people going about their daily bath room routines, ever give thought to the fact that they must be made somewhere. And sold by someone. I launched a campaign that took a sympathetic-but-humorous view of the life of a toilet seat salesman. Mimi listened patiently as I excitedly related the pure genius behind this campaign to help my client dominate the toilet seat market.

Eleven-year-old daughter, Linda, was listening too. In the dark of her room that night, we heard soft sobbing.

"What's wrong?", we asked.

"I don't want Daddy to sell toilet seats!" she blurted out.

As we comforted her, we learned of her disillusionment and fear at this latest turn in Dad's career. She and little sister Angela had visited me at my corporate digs. How could I trade all this for peddling potty seats?

Think higher. It's task master and tear jerker. I would make them all proud – and secure – some day.

■ ■ ■

Meetings always bored me

Our plane was landing. Time for one of the first big tests of my worth to an important client. Failure now would raise my own doubts about the wisdom of my Kamstra Communications venture. Client meetings would concentrate on finding ways to counter the omnipotent and dominant presence of Xerox in the market place. I would be expected to give a creative edge to whatever marketing or sales strategies that would come from these meetings. Heady stuff.

The client's division vice president – a God-like position in this company – opened the meeting with an overview of Xerox's growing market dominance. Then he skillfully articulated his company's newfound competitive edge, primarily a price advantage. It wasn't – at least for a seasoned journalist – a difficult situation to grasp. Yet, the pros and cons of how to proceed against Xerox were hashed and rehashed into the afternoon and, finally, a merciful adjournment.

Next day, we started all over again. I slid into my chair, determined to pay close attention. To take notes even when nothing of significance was being said. About mid morning, an energetic young regional manager offered a highly optimistic opinion.

"I think Xerox is a sitting duck on this one."

For two days, I had been tuning in and out of the meetings as they droned on. I felt somewhat guilty since my client was paying me a substantial fee for sitting in on this meeting, not to mention all expenses.

Still meetings always bored me. People take forever to get to the point. What's more, they often seem unclear about what the point is. So far, I only knew for sure that the enemy was Xerox. I knew first hand about competitive selling. It seemed simple enough to me; just get the salesmen off their asses and after those guys at Xerox who are eating their lunch. I spelled out the word on my place mat; it worked better for sketching and doodling than my tiny note pad.

XEROX   XEROX   XEROX   XEROX   XEROX   XEROX

Nice name. Doesn't really say anything, but powerful. People use it generically to the consternation of its owner. Still, in offices across America, people were saying, "better make a Xerox of this" or "I'll send you a Xerox of the memo." Not a bad position for a company to be in.

Wait a minute! Wait just a darn minute! What did the speaker just say? He said "Xerox is a sitting duck." That means vulnerable to attack. Maybe complacent, sluggish, slow to respond. Like…like…an…

…an ox! THE ZEER OX. THE GOLDEN OX. THE GOLDEN OX FROM THE LAND OF ZEER.

You have to be a little crazy

You have be a little crazy – not just unorthodox – to make your living as an "idea person". This, I firmly believed, was an idea that for all its craziness would fly. Well, maybe lumber along, but still fly. The "Golden Ox" would become the focal point – the fun focal point – for everyone, particularly salesmen, who made their living competing with Xerox. It was the kind of concept that would become the hallmark of a "Kamstra Brand" sales promotion program.

In minutes, I went from boredom to obsession. As the meetings dragged on, I was sketching – crudely in spite of my art training – the nucleus of a story board. This, I envisioned, would be the center piece of a comprehensive program to fire up a sales force for a take-no-prisoners attack on Xerox.

Back in the Twin Cities, I jumped in my car – soon to be upgraded – and headed for my favorite art studio. I was an agency with no staff, but close working relations with some of the most talented graphic arts people around. I handed them a bundle of notes, scribbled napkins and sketches… and a 48-hour deadline. Parlaying a core idea to every conceivable communication, I included a concept for a national sales meeting, a "Royal Oxblood Society" (for salesmen meeting "Ox kill" minimums), a series of "Oxiom" mailers (ageless wisdom regarding Ox hunting) and more.

So certain of client approval was I, that I assumed thousands of dollars in art costs without once touching bases with the client. After the marathon meetings ended, I had only been assigned to come up with a one-color cost comparison brochure.

The "Golden Ox" was born

Two days later, I presented my "Golden Ox" concept to the client. They were shocked at my audacity but absolutely ecstatic. When a client truly wraps his arms around your idea, there is no thrill quite like it. In a matter of days, the idea went from the client's ad people to sales management, marketing management and ultimately top management. I had achieved company wide acceptance of a crazy-but-logical motivational program.

"This pulls our national sales meeting together with one idea," said the division vice president. Without his buy-in, an idea can die in infancy.

Sales-promotion-intensive agencies like mine had to learn to live on the edge; minus the security of monthly fees enjoyed by conventional, ad-oriented agencies. But I had the last laugh. Management was far less tight fisted when it came to spending money on programs that immediately sweetened the bottom line. They found money their agencies-of-record didn't even know existed

Before the hundreds of salesmen and management people converged on Sun Valley for their national "After The Ox" sales meeting, the program just kept growing and enlarging. Without staff or overhead, my income for the program dwarfed anything I could have imagined just a year or two earlier.

"Think Higher. Never be satisfied with where you are today!" I declared to myself (there being no one else with whom to share this wisdom.) "Always give clients more than they expect; get 'emotionally involved' in helping them reach their goals".

This would be my lifelong philosophy.

And here I was in Sun Valley like a director watching his movie unfold. Every attendee was presented with a pewter mug – appropriately wrapped in "ox hide" – and later filled with "ox blood"; actually a giant bloody Mary. We toasted the occasion with songs and "Oxioms" on into the boisterous closing hours of the final banquet.

"I think if a Xerox salesman walked into the room right now, he would be torn limb from limb", the national sales manager confided to me.

I just nodded and grinned. Ken Kamstra had found his life's work.

■ ■ ■

Ken Kamstra had found his life's work

CHAPTER 17

Does God Hate Porsches?

Francine was convinced; certain that God took a dim view of man's inclination to indulge his baser desires. Desires like strong drink, frivolous sex and self indulgent worldly goods.

"That Porsche has got to go!"

"That Porsche has to go!" she proclaimed with an air of authority that only wives can voice. Even young, newly wed wives. Francine and Bernard had been married only a few weeks. Still, there was no question about who would be wearing the pants in this family.

Not cleansed of all impure thoughts myself, the image of Francine wearing – or not wearing – pants conjured up some shameful lust in my mind.

Francine stood at the kitchen stove in their immaculate trailer house. She was brewing coffee for me and her obviously obedient hubby. Her tight-jeans-clad derriere suggested to my prurient mind that Bernard would not be foregoing all worldly pleasures.

But the Porsche was not to be one of those pleasures. For this couple, life would be dictated by strict born-again Christian principles. Wherever there was wall space in their compact trailer house, another portrait of Jesus looked benignly down on us. I tried to discipline my mind to only the purest, most pious thoughts.

Bernard, a shy, gangly youth, said very little as we sat at the cozy table filling out papers that would transfer his once proud possession to me. As he filled in the information – in what must have been agonizing moments – I thought back to the tiny want ad that had caught my eye just the day before. The ad read:

> FOR SALE- Near new Porsche 356B cabriolet. 2300 actual miles. Must sell Call XXX-XXXX after 5.

To me the ad screamed:

> ATTENTION, KEN KAMSTRA!
> YOUR PORSCHE HAS COME IN!

Kicking and screaming on the inside

Bernard wrote. I drooled. The Jesus-taunting-orange-red Porsche convertible sat just outside, framed in the picture window that is standard equipment on every trailer house ever built. I knew about trailer houses, later to be called "mobile homes". My newlywed years had been spent in one; 18 feet long and well used. There were another 50 or so nondescript trailer homes in the trailer park. Bernard's was the only one with a brand new 356 Porsche parked next to it. Bernard – trying to prove he had balls even though he was about to surrender his Porsche – demanded something close to new list price: $3,600. No problem. I had already worked it out with the bank; Bernard got my check. Sin was cheaper in 1961. Class-envy-bating politicians hadn't yet invented the "luxury tax", gas guzzler tax or license plate fees based on how much you paid for your wheels.

My state of mind was nearing irrational, babbling euphoria. I could only imagine what Bernard's state of mind must have been. Poor Bernard – Francine called him "my Bernie" – had only driven the Porsche from the Port of Entry in New Jersey to St. Paul's east side. America was not dotted with Porsche dealers in 1961; buyers had to order them imported. For Bernard's sake, I hoped every mile he drove from New Jersey had been pure ecstasy.

Bernard was, after all, a fellow AED addict.

Now the Porsche was mine. My first real sportscar ever. A fitting "company car" for the fledgling, flamboyant Kamstra Communications ad agency; albeit an agency still sharing space with the basement laundry room.

Kicking and screaming on the inside perhaps, Bernard was nonetheless divesting himself of hedonistic, worldly possessions. I, on the other hand, was – belatedly at 35 – just entering an era where some serious automotive hedonism was within reach. It was a classic example of being in the right place at the right time. Bernard was renouncing; Ken Kamstra was indulging and accumulating.

Let Saint Peter judge me harshly in the Great Beyond, this beautiful fall day, I was going to own a real Porsche.

Bernard followed me in the Porsche. I drove the Kamstra "family car", actually my "pretend sportscar", a Studebaker coupe, back to our home. This was a

> *The little Porsche would change my life forever*

milestone event in my life. I would, as the years of AED addiction unfolded, own other, more exotic, more expensive cars, but the thrill wouldn't quite measure up to this first prize. When we arrived at my home, I considered parking the Porsche Jewel in my driveway, then taking Bernard back to his trailer park in the old Studebaker. No. That would have been inhumane. Something one Auto Erotic does not do to another .

"You drive me back. Maybe you can give me a few tips on how to handle her," I said with as much compassion as I could muster.

Bernard retained command of the magnificent red machine. I took the navigator's seat. He didn't offer any driving tips. In fact, neither of us spoke. Still, I think we bonded somewhat.

Meanwhile, as I knew it would, the little Porsche would change my life forever. It would put an end to any chance that I might outgrow my AED affliction. Fine with me; I didn't want it to end. Mimi, my ever tolerant wife, might have hoped I would come to accept a sensible station wagon like my Auto Immune neighbors, but she didn't push it. We did have some rules: (1) mortgage payments, groceries and other necessities took priority over sportscar payments, (2) the Studebaker "family car" got the one garage stall.

Rain, snow or sleet – standard fare for Minnesota – the 356 would make its home on a strip of land beside our driveway. Reading this, new generation auto buffs might consider this sacrilege. I rationalized it as pragmatism; knowing how to live with an Auto Immune spouse. Not incidentally, a spouse who was also pretty, sexy and one helluva good cook. Even a seriously addicted AED has to keep some sense of perspective. Besides, how was I to know the 356 would one day be a sought after collector's car. This was an era when new gullwing Mercedes sportscars or new Ferraris could be bought for under $20,000.

Who knew – or cared – which cars would some day become classics. In truth, I was probably more Philistine than Porschephile at this stage in my life. Just having car fun; compensating for decades of poverty. I got a late start. Later still because I was born at the wrong time "warwise"; Navy hitches in World War II and Korea before the age of 30. My self pity for this life interruption was cut short when I realized that old Doctor Ferdinand Porsche fared far worse. He spent years in a French prison dungeon as part of his penalty for World War II.

Nonetheless, he was able to create the first 356 Porsche and mastermind some of its evolution before his death in 1951. Surely Ferdinand Porsche and his son, Ferry, were living examples of the positive good that can come of AED affliction. Surely, too, God couldn't have been totally displeased with their life long crusade to bring so much auto erotic pleasure to so many.

Now. Now, no matter how the serious Christians might scorn my behavior, I was on a roll. And this little Porsche rag top was going to help me roll in style.

Smash the pedal; sooth the soul!

As the 356 daily fulfilled my AED cravings, I thought once more of Bernard and Francine. I genuinely hoped that someday Francine might relent. Maybe she would ask God to rethink his policy on Porsches.

■ ■ ■

Would God reconsider one day?

Author Ken with first Porsche and second daughter: 356B Cabriolet and Angela Dawn.

CHAPTER 18

The Unpampered Porsche

The "morning after" brought nary a pang of conscience or buyer's regret. The child within me tugged us to the front window of our modest home. There it was! It was not a dream! It was real! My very first sportscar! The little red "inverted bath tub", officially the Porsche 356B Cabriolet.

It was not a dream!

A momentary flash from somewhere in the memory bank of my brain took me back to one of the many "renter farms" of my childhood. My family's cashless existence meant that Christmas morning gifts often consisted of a new pair of long john winter underwear or other country living necessities. This Christmas morning was going to be different, filled with anticipation for me. When I was supposed to be sound asleep, I had sneaked to the head of the stairs and watched as my older brothers gleefully assembled a big red open touring car. The toy – maybe 18 inches long and sporting rubber tires – seemed to fascinate them as much as it did me. It was a wind up machine with tiny, battery powered bulbs in front for headlights. Lord knows where they came up with the money.

It had to be for me; I was the only male Kamstra not present at the Christmas 'Eve assembly session. I knew it wasn't for my sisters; their tough luck. My six-year-old heart was pounding. Could this have been an early symptom of AED? The next morning's unveiling – we didn't waste funds on holiday wrapping – was only slightly less rapturous than last night's anticipation. Long-john-clad family members – we didn't waste money on pajamas or bathrobes either – were gathered around the big, pot bellied "parlor furnace". I headed straight for the big red car, bursting with joyous anticipation.

Both headlights were broken and the grill was smashed!

Seems the car had been "drive tested" too thoroughly by the Kamstra assembly crew. Too young for tact, I cried openly and accusingly as I looked up at my older brothers. I wanted to say, "you bastards!". They, too, had known few real toys in their childhood; and they were undoubtedly reliving their own childhoods as they "tested" the car last night. The car must have gotten away from them on one run. And, of course, they must have sacrificed or sold something to buy this one toy for skinny little "Kenny". That kind of compassion and understanding is foreign to a six-year-old. In minutes, however, I was enthralled with this my first toy car not fashioned out of cast off farm machinery. My imagination had already concocted death-defying crash episodes that explained the front end damage.

Now I was looking out the window at the real thing; and there was no former owner damage inflicted by Bernard.

"Orange-red is a great color for catching the morning sun", I said to myself. And this was one Porsche that would be one with the sun. And with the wind and the rain and the first frost and the ice and the inevitable snow. Home for this Porsche – I dubbed it "Little Red" – would be a skinny strip of land that separated my driveway from the next door neighbor. He was an Auto Immune who drove a big, sensible Buick station wagon. Bought a new one every other year. Had a high paying engineer's job and looked with scarcely concealed scorn on the outlandish promotional schemes I was creating for my clients. We became next-door-neighbor-friends. He was probably looking out his window about now and thinking "more damn foolishness."

No matter how anyone viewed Little Red, a garage-less outdoors would be its operational world. I suspected that old Ferdinand Porsche designed this car – it was his first sportscar too – for unpampered, drive-'em-like-hell duty. As he master minded the evolution of the 356, he wasted precious little time engineering a heater that would actually keep the driver from freezing at the wheel. The good "Doktor" thought heaters were for wimps.

Sun-baked California wimps might have given Little Red a less punishing existence. So would rich collectors who could pick and choose just the right kind of day to exercise a prize Porsche like mine. My Porsche was to be a company car; a work-every-day-no-matter-what car. Economics dictated this philosophy for the present, but I would never relinquish it. My "pizza case", art-carrying hallmark of any adman worth his salt, could be shoe-horned into the front cargo space, resting on the spare tire. This would be a car to inspire many a "Golden Ox" idea.

Company car or whatever, I couldn't wait to fire it up. This was going to be sustained auto eroticism. Dr. Geernoggin would be pleased.

"Little Red"

Little Red made hustling a lot more fun

A tug at my bathrobe snapped me out of my euphoria. This time, it wasn't my inner child. It was my real child. Eight year old Angela Dawn. We named her that because she was born at dawn and we just knew she was going to be an angel. One of the many injustices of life is that kids must go through it with names conjured up by parental whim. At least we didn't call her "Chastity" or "Latrina."

Angela loved early morning as much as I did. Her favorite toy was an "Etch-A-Sketch" we bought her for her third birthday; two dials and a screen on which to draw stuff. No computer wizardry; just two-handed talent. Every morning, she'd tippy toe out of bed to simultaneously watch cartoons and create ever more credible sketches on her magic art machine. So engrossed was she that she was oblivious to my entering the room. When I could, I would watch TV with her. "Dudley Do-Right" was our favorite. Angela never lost her inventive wonder as she matured to womanhood and ultimately her own studio, turning out books, games and art for kids.

"Dad," she said, continuing to tug at my robe until I put my arm around her and we both gazed out at the gleaming new Porsche. She didn't have to say more. She knew about toys and the joys they bring.

Daughter, Linda, at 13 was more inclined to stay in bed as long as possible before it was off to school. She was the more analytical one but nonetheless thrilled to have a Porsche in the family. Both girls had to find a way to squeeze into the laughable rear seats of Little Red. It was part of the price children pay when dad's AED affliction enters more advanced stages. Later in life, as a psychologist, she has been known to question whether AED is a legitimate disease or merely a manifestation of arrested adolescence. I say who is she to question the legendary Dr. Geernoggin.

Little Red and I became inseparable. Not a surprising statement when you consider we went everywhere together. Hustling, I had long ago learned, is the key to business success and an absolute necessity to supporting a family. Little Red made hustling a lot more fun.

■ ■ ■

The sun was just peeking over the rolling hills of southern Minnesota as Red and I were making our way to visit the Maytag folks in Newton, Iowa. Maytag, of course, was a big, famous, international company. Still, I found them to be just folks in a small town. Dependable products that would never let you down was their thing. You could sense it as you walked through the plants and chatted in the unpretentious offices of the marketing, sales and advertising people.

Their way of portraying this dependability to the world was and is one of the most simply brilliant communications concepts of all time. Who hasn't sympathized with the "lonely repairman" bored to tears waiting in vain for the service call that never comes. Who among the world's advertising great would not secretly admit that – faced with the same opportunity – they might have opted to try to explain the superior inner mechanics of Maytag machines.

"Wish I had thought of the Maytag repairman!" I shouted into the wind rushing over my top-down chariot.

Nonetheless, I had convinced Maytag to hire me for some of their sales promotion projects. Less glamorous and high profile than worldwide ad campaigns, but a pleasing and profitable addition to the Kamstra Communications client list. Just because my headquarters were of the home basement variety, was no reason not to seek out the biggest and best clients. I was determined not to become one of the nameless, faceless free lancers frittering away their lives on no-name, no-challenge clients.

Red and I were going places. We would take the back roads but never the low roads. Truth is, out of town clients always received an extra measure of attention from me. Simple AED logic. These were Porsche-intensive clients. The road to Newton, for instance – depending on which of my special routes I chose – was a bit under or just over 300 miles of Porsche paradise. Roller coaster hills, "S" curves, fun roads. Roads where you could stake out the best home made pecan rolls and coffee. One had to start out well before breakfast to reach Newton "the creative way" and still be on time for a late morning meeting. Little Red topped out at a mere 100 mph, but it got the job done.

Porsche-intensive clients

The "Prairie Rambler" reincarnated

We had just mounted one of the more gut satisfying hills when it hit me.

"The Prairie Rambler! Yee Haaaa!"

Red stayed glued to the blacktop, asking from me only an occasional flick of the steering wheel. Gave me time to think. Had I reincarnated the "Prairie Rambler" concept; the one abandoned at birth in Huron, South Dakota? Could it be that ideas continue to germinate and evolve in the recesses of the mind without conscious involvement of the mind's owner? True, I was no longer a journalist roaming the Dakota prairies in search of human interest stories. But, damned if I wasn't rolling across Minnesota/Iowa prairies seeking out potential business success stories. "Human interest" stories of humans who were trying their best to beat the hell out of competition. And I was trying to help them do just that.

For me, it was far more rewarding to involve myself in the outcome of stories than to merely observe and report them. Most important to my struggle to live with AED, I held onto "my space". Found a way to make a living – a darn good living – without surrendering to corporate confinement. I had escaped the employee regimentation that is an essential part of operating a business or any other kind of institution.

I was doing my own thing. Doing it my way. Administering to my AED affliction. I could go anywhere, anytime so long as I brought home the bacon and a few extra bucks for the bills. Millions of miles of soul-satisfying back roads beckon the AED's among us. This addict was rapidly learning how these roads can lead to both fun and profit.

It's not always easy fun. You satisfy – hopefully enthuse – clients or else. "Else" being a return to more conventional, payroll-dependent work and maybe week-ends-only car buffery. I was building an impressive roster of clients who liked my unconventional-but-profit-logical approach. With each successful project, it seemed more certain that this maverick could roam free and still be accepted, even welcomed, as a source of valuable business counsel and service. The folks at Maytag usually liked my ideas. They even put me on the coveted mailing list for bleu cheese from the famous Maytag Farms. My day had started at 5; the drive back would be long but fun; deciphering my client notes wouldn't. It would be another one of those 16 hour days; maybe 17. Not easy, but right then I wouldn't trade jobs with anyone. Not even Maytag's CEO in the big corner office.

■ ■ ■

Little Red, the weight of its hefty little engine bearing down on its rear wheels, turned out to be a pretty good snow car. Even after the indignity of a night parked in the oil-congealing cold, it would usually start with a couple of grunting turns of the starter.

One day, December 31, 1963 to be exact, Red and I were up and off early, making our rounds of client calls. December was always a panic month. Not holiday parties; pressure. Through summer and fall, many clients couldn't or wouldn't get serious about the coming new year.

"I wake up New Year's Day and I am already behind forecast," as one of my many sales manager friends remarked.

Nonetheless, December was always the month when clients and their service agencies paid the price for earlier procrastination. What's more, many clients were sweating out the loss of promotional budgets if they lapsed into the new year unspent. The major year end challenge for most was the traditional January sales meeting. The ritual that brings together regional, national and even international sales forces. Much conviviality, too much booze, too many dull speeches, grandiose "new/improved" product introductions and more. Often, these meetings would take place in warm places, even cruise ships. It was management's way of simultaneously expressing appreciation for last year's efforts and demonstrating how good life can be for the successful sales person.

These events were my specialty; a specialty most conventional ad agencies were happy to relinquish as one big pain in the butt that was better done by someone else. I enjoyed the work. Liked tying it all together under one theme. "We need a mission not just a motto," I would implore them. More and more, motivation intrigued me. It was the "X Factor" in human performance which in turn became the "X Factor" driving some companies to leave their bewildered

"We need a mission, not just a motto"

competitors in the dust. I liked to think my interest in the subject was intensified by my personal battles to overcome poverty and a self-inflicted lack of education.

Sales related programs were the backbone and the bread and butter of fledgling Kamstra Communications in the those early years. Two of my favorite prejudices were (1) that every copywriter should begin his career as a what-in-the-hell-is-the-story journalist and (2) every aspiring agency should have first hand knowledge of the real world selling process.

"Nothing happens until somebody sells something!" Whoever first said that nailed it. Because most client management understands this principle, they always have money tucked away for stimulating sales. "Agencies of record" never got their hands on these bucks; but I did. Ah the life of a sales motivation maverick.

Funding yes. Time no. From strategy meetings to finished product was a torturous ordeal. Everything needed to be done: speech writing, audio visual blockbusters, pre-and-post-meeting mailers, sales literature, sales aids and on and on. Little Red and I criss-crossed the Minneapolis/St. Paul "Twin Cities" urging artists and myriad graphic arts craftsmen to work faster. Chastising, pleading, paying overtime. Whatever it took to meet deadlines.

And then it was the final day of the final month of December. As always, there were some programs and pieces yet to be put in the hands of waiting clients. Clients anxious for their programs and for departing flight schedules that would give them a break from Minnesota frigid to golf country warm.

New Year's Eve was only hours away. Forecasters were predicting temperatures that might plummet to 30 below this night. Windchills could hit 50 below! These are the temperatures that can freeze human flesh in under five minutes. Minnesota Rule One: don't get caught out in this stuff.

Little Red had performed magnificently every day that I owned her; and today was no exception. The 356 "heater" didn't affect freezing temperatures inside the car. It did clear a grapefruit-sized arc in the frosted windshield, permitting cautious forward navigation. Winter days like this triggered in me a grudging envy of Auto Immune motorists who sailed by in their over-sized,

Don't get caught out in this stuff

toasty warm Detroit iron. The envy was only aggravated by the stark awareness that only an idiot or an AED addict would try to maintain a sports car enthusiast's lifestyle through Minnesota winters. I would, of course, never reveal these thoughts to anyone. Neither would I confess to any client that I might covet their expense-account-funded escape. Sometimes, I was invited to come along but usually that privilege was reserved for their "real agency" whose head honcho would give a speech intimating that he had some idea of what was going on.

I wasn't going to Florida but I was going to the bank. It had been a good year for my little, one-maverick shop. These thoughts warmed my brain but did nothing for my shivering body as I trudged back to Little Red, waiting for me in the client parking lot. It was late; coming on 6 p.m. Employees and "vendors" – I hated being called a "vendor" – had mostly vanished. Little Red looked forlorn and out of place sitting alone as powdery snow whipped around it. Soon, though, its little four-cylinder heart would be doing its "plugga, plugga" beat again and we would be heading to a warm house, even warmer hugs from Mimi and the girls and maybe a cool Scotch – or two – before dinner. And who knows what other delights of domesticity before this New Year's Eve was over.

The Porsche door creaked and cracked as I opened it. In this temperature, everything turns brittle; even people. I shut the door against the cold. A twist of the key and we would be on our way. The client-to-client marathon would be over for this year. A twist of the key and…

> …nothing! Nothing but a sickly "errump, errump" followed by an all too familiar "click, click" of a frozen battery telling me "I just ain't gonna' take it anymore!"

These are the sounds that strike terror in the heart of even the most hardened and dedicated Minnesotan. Now what? Would my career and my life end in this ignoble manner? Car phones didn't exist then at least for me. From a nearby pay phone I relearned what I already knew: when temperatures head for 20 or 30 below, every towing service, cab company or other source of rescue is swamped. Help, if any, is hours away. Time enough for flesh – and bone – to freeze quite solid.

"Errump, errump"

Whimpering, begging and "forced entry"

Just then, a lumbering tow truck drove into view, heading right for me and Little Red. A thoughtful, life saving – and free – service provided by my client for employees and vendors alike. I was towed to a nearby service station. Help at last! I was saved! Soon the two teenagers manning the station would compassionately push Little Red into one of their warm service bays. Red would be thawed out in no time and we'd be off for home.

"No way!" said the teenager without a hint of empathy for a fellow human in need. It was pointed out in compassion-less terms that many other frozen cars – cars owned by regular customers – would be thawed out ahead of mine.

"But they're not here. They're already home enjoying their New Year's Eve! I have to get home. Please!" I was whimpering and begging now. I hated people who do that. Besides, I was being ignored.

"We close at eight and that's just 20 minutes from now", the teen-in-charge said, annoyed by my presence and my persistence. "You'd better call a cab." These young men bore no resemblance to the crisply uniformed, always smiling, always helpful attendants portrayed in oil company ads. They were closing; they had New Year's parties coming up. This was my problem, not theirs. Cab companies had ceased to answer their phones, even to tell you there was no way they could help.

Fear and panic set in. I could freeze to death huddled next to my beloved Porsche and nobody in this station would really give a damn. Auto Immunes!

Just then a well dressed young man pulled up to the pumps for gas. He was alone, slight of stature. And he had a nice warm car that was running and had plenty of room for a passenger. I decided it would be me.

Opening his passenger door, I stood there; all 6 feet, 200 pounds of me. My oversized mustache hung with ice and so did my attitude. No longer the skinny guy of my youth, I looked like I could hurt somebody if I chose to. I never have hurt anyone even in my short lived stint at boxing in the Navy. The young driver didn't know that, of course. A look of sheer terror crossed his face as I slid into the seat beside him.

"If you can't take me home, at least take me to someplace warm," I said trying to explain my plight but making it clear by my tone of voice that I had no intention of taking no for an answer. I wasn't leaving his car until my chances for survival had vastly improved.

Fear obvious in his voice, he mumbled something about having a New Year's date. Then we were off. Ten minutes later, we pulled up in front of what he said was his girl friend's house, insisting he must explain to her why their date would be delayed. Seemed a reasonable request to me, especially since it was, after all, his car.

Still, I wondered. Would he come charging out with a bunch of his full-back-sized buddies? Would they beat me up and throw me in a snow bank to freeze after all? Or might he call the cops and tell 'em he's holding a "car jacker". It seemed an eternity until the young man returned. Alone. He asked for more complete directions to my home and you could have heard my sigh of relief across town.

A few miles later, we pulled into my driveway. Never had my home looked so sweet. I thanked him profusely and apologized for intruding on his evening. Then I handed him all the money I had in my wallet, twenty two dollars. Twenty bucks was more serious spending money in 1963. I hoped he would spend it on his girl friend. She probably dissuaded him from calling the cops.

I sometimes wonder how many times he has retold and embellished the story of the hulking, half-frozen brute who took command of his car.

As the warmth of my home thawed body and brain, while the Scotch warmed my insides, I felt an extra appreciation that I would live to see another year.

During the night's ordeal, visions of my clients winging their way south, rehearsing the words of speeches I had written while I froze to death in some crummy service station did stir some resentment. Totally unfair and irrational resentment, since they paid me well, but resentment just the same.

Sip by sip, the Scotch washed the resentment away. Happy New Year!

> *I would live to see another year*

■ ■ ■

CHAPTER 19

Parking Paranoia:
Terror In The Buff

Keeweenie Cargoyle®: cult hero

The battle is bloodless – except for the occasional crazies – and it is wordless too. It goes on every day, all day, far into the night, seven days a week. The battle ground is America's parking lots and ramps; the antagonists come from two car cultures destined to be forever opposed. They occasionally glare at each other but will never see eye to eye.

Car affectionados, those with the AED Gene and with their prerequisite pristinely polished autos, see the Auto Immune parkers as door-dinging, fender-scrunching, insensitive louts. Secretly, they envy the Auto Immune; envy the way they nonchalantly squeeze into any available parking space, never giving it a second thought.

As the hapless car lover cruises frantically and fruitlessly in search of that secure, ding-safe parking space, he must suffer the indignity of watching hordes of Auto Immune parkers burst out of their vehicles in carefree pursuit of their daily affairs. Mostly, these Auto Immunes are blissfully unaware that there is another car culture out there; a culture of paranoid perfectionists who would walk extra blocks and endure any hardship to safeguard their sacred cars. If the Auto Immune were to think of the auto freaks at all, they would see us as just that – freaks, foppish freaks, conspicuous consumers and probably God awful Republicans to boot.

Actually, the Auto Immune harbor a fringe cult of their own. This group feeds on the terror in the hearts of the AED afflicted parkers. Starting in earliest puberty, they share – and sharpen – their harassment techniques. They have their own cult hero, the "Keeweenie" Cargoyle (see next page); their own underground newspaper, *The Dingers Digest,* and their own vernacular. To the dinger, for instance, a "four banger" is not a four cylinder car but a clunker with four doors. This four door is the dinger's assault weapon; the civilian equivalent of the military Hummer vehicle. Load it with kids or any kind of mean spirited passengers, and they can inflict multiple classic car battery, port and starboard.

Some of the more dedicated dingers still insist that a two door, one with a seven foot door span, can be just as lethal in the hands of a skilled parking lot demolition expert. The Keeweenie is, of course, smug in his knowledge that you don't even need a car to terrorize car buffs. Debates on this and like subjects enliven the pages of each issue of *Dingers Digest,* contributing to its loyal readership. Rumor has it that a consortium of auto body shops actually founded and supports the *Digest.* This, however, has never been proven.

How do we fight back? Those of us who have been ding victims know that even the most skilled auto body repairmen cannot totally restore the ravaged surface. We might believe it on the joyous day we reclaim our beloved toy with its telltale banana oil aroma. But some day later, while we are still paying off the bill, the sunlight will catch the repainted surface just right. There, for God and everyone to see, will be the ghost of the damnable ding!

So widespread is the ding epidemic that a new profession has been born: ding surgery. Specialists now work from deep within the hidden inner cavities of your car to extract the ding without repainting. It should not surprise you that the skills – and the bills – of these practitioners rival that of brain surgeons. Many actually are brain surgeons. They are merely hedging their bets on career options should the specter of Hillary Rodham Clinton's one-doctor's-salary-fits-all health plan once more rears its ugly head.

Maybe, instead of paying brain surgeon rates to fix our car bodies, we should pay psychiatrists to fix our heads. It might require a costly series of sessions, maybe even hypnosis. Still, if it worked, we could then drive our cars – and park them – anywhere, everywhere, every day. Just say to hell with worrying about it. There is that AED Gene, however. I've never met a car addict who has successfully altered it.

A less expensive alternative – actually preferred by most car lovers – is to buy a beater. With it, you can infiltrate the ranks of the auto immune. Join them in their glorious state of carefree abandon. Park anywhere; do anything. You would, of course, be abandoning the car you love. It would mean relegating that regal, gleaming masterpiece of the auto makers art to only an occasional Sunday sprint.

AED addiction has no cure, no easy answers. But aren't you glad you suffer with it?

> *AED addiction has no cure, no easy answers*

Keeweenie

Think of the Keeweenie as the guerrilla terrorist of America's self imposed class warfare. The sight of your highly polished car ignites a gleam in his beady little eyes. Envy! Rage! Revenge against an unjust society; one that would deny him a car as fine as yours. Nothing personal, you understand, it's just the inequality of it all. Then comes the attack. Swift. Sure. Deep. You have been "keyed" by the dreaded Keeweenie. To add insult to injury, he may actually pause to preen in the mirror finish of your car before loping off. Try to be philosophic; you still have your car. ■ Caution: the Keeweenie is a protected species under the Disadvantaged and Underprivileged Minors (D.U.M.) act. It is unlawful to capture a Keeweenie. D.U.M. officials further warn that using harsh or abusive language against a Keeweenie could permanently damage their self esteem. Either offense is punishable by confiscation of your car.

■ ■ ■

He lopes, he lurks;
his brain is teeny
a fearsome lout
they call Keyweenie

Don't park your car
where he might see it.
He'll sneak and snicker,
then he'll "key" it.

Valet parking; wherein Lead-Foot takes your wheels

One recurring, real life nightmare of auto-buffery is the dreaded parking attendant, sometimes called a "valet". Many of society's most malevolent youth find their way to this occupation. The attraction is obvious: hours of inactivity interspersed with "performance testing" other people's cars while simultaneously intimidating the cars' owners.

If you are rich or on an expense account, you can circumvent the problem. Simply press some large bills into the eager hand of the attendant. Said attendant will then ease your chariot into a place of honor just steps from the front door of El Affluenza Restaurante. With one flourish of a handful of money, you have purchased peace of mind during your dinner while establishing your status in the eyes of the less fortunate outside, still waiting to arrange parking.

The Auto Immune fare almost as well, peace-of-mindwise, but without the ego satisfaction. Indifferent to the motorized appliance in which they have arrived, they are oblivious to the indignities – if not out outright damage – about to befall their car. As a final irony, they will probably overtip the attendant in a vain effort to assure better parking or retrieval next time.

Then you show up in your pristine 356 Porsche, for instance. To the attendant, it's just another little red sports car. And who the hell are you anyway? Your attendant, a rebellious individual who may be male, female, or somewhere in between, never heard of a 356 and couldn't care less. You try to break through the generation gap; start some dialog.

"Can I park it myself?"

"Not allowed."

"Is there another lot nearby?"

"No."

"Can you leave it up front with these other cars?" you ask, extending a hand openly revealing a $5 bill.

"Spaces all taken."

You and your lady are by now starving. You relent and hand over the keys to your gleaming red jewel. Parking attendants are mostly Auto Immune, too. They don't know about clutches and shifting. Just as you're entering the restaurant, you hear the piercing scream of your helpless little Porsche. A sick feeling comes over you. You have betrayed your pact of love with the Porsche of your dreams. While you are contemplating food and wine, your loved one out there in the dark is being brutalized by a barbarian.

Suddenly, you're not hungry anymore.

> *A sick feeling comes over you*

CHAPTER 20

Joe Livinhi; Still Out There Somewhere, Everywhere

You have indeed arrived, or have you?

Maybe it was the previous night's terror in my frozen 356 Porsche, but some of my New Year's Day reflections focused on the phenomenon of expense account high living. I'll never forget my first exposure to this life style and, in retrospect, never stop wondering what this phenomenon really costs America or any country advanced enough to engage in it. My concern is not that of our demagogic politicians. Masters of the art themselves, they wring their hands over the "three martini lunch"; worry that evil American business people might be catching up.

I worry about the real cost: the dulling and ultimate death of one's entrepreneurial drive. It is difficult, after all, to sustain this drive – and its inherent demand for self discipline and sacrifice – when circumstances offer you immediate entry into the hallowed halls of high living. Qualifications for entry are few and, with a little self deception, you can convince yourself that you have indeed arrived. At the very least, you can believe that you are definitely on your way.

■ ■ ■

My first invitation came from a Baltimore businessman .

"How would you like to join me for dinner tonight?" he asked, beaming with good natured hospitality. He was a pudgy, friendly, fiftyish guy; an outspoken, often profane CEO of his own distribution business. He was outstripping competition in rate of growth, profit margins and just about every other success criteria .

This is what brought me to Baltimore to interview him. I was here to uncover his success secrets for my publisher boss and maybe myself. Earlier in the day, I had done an interview in Chicago and another was scheduled for Washington, D.C., the next day. Heady stuff for a still skinny guy in his twenties. In spite of the "big time" city visits, however, I was still a bumpkin when it came to expense accounts. Budget hotels and family restaurants were my style; much, I am sure, to the delight of my boss.

"Sure," I responded, almost too eagerly, "I would be glad to have dinner with you. I don't have a tie or a jacket with me, though. Will that be a problem?"

"No problem!", Sam (not his real name) responded without hesitation, simultaneously motioning for me to follow him out to his parking lot.

"I don't have a tie or a sport coat or a suit back at my hotel either," I thought to myself, stuffing interview notes into my pocket as I followed Sam out to his car. Retaining my Daily Plainsman news reporting dress code, I still wore my small town reporter's garb: shirt, slacks and slightly scruffy loafers. In time, I would realize that if you look like you're nobody, that's probably who you will be .

I wanted to be somebody. Poverty, I learned first hand, is no damn fun. Being with rich and successful entrepreneurs like Sam fueled my ambition and helped to give it definition. How fortunate for this ambition that I was actually being paid to snoop into the secrets of the super successful.

Sam had one secret that wouldn't find its way into my story. She was tall, taller than Sam, and definitely statuesque. We, Sam and I, picked her up at her apartment a couple of miles or so from Sam's office. As a newspaper reporter, I had worked with prosecuting attorneys investigating everything from illegal abortion dens to mysterious deaths. I liked investigative reporting but Sam's plot was elementary. I was about to be convenient "cover" for his night out with Susie (not her real name). We all rode in the front seat of Sam's battle-ship-sized Cadillac convertible.

The evening began with drinks at a trendy all black jazz bar. Once inside, I was glad to be without tie or jacket. The mostly black patrons didn't seem all that hospitable toward rich whites invading their turf. I definitely didn't look like a rich white. Sam did. Susie seemed uneasy. Both black and white patrons were leering at her provocatively packaged charms.

"I'll have a rum and coke," I said to the burly bartender. It was a hold over from my Navy days in Cuba where everyone seemed to drink rum and coke. Others in the bar probably saw it as still further evidence that there was a white nerd in their midst. I was enjoying my drink, the jazz I didn't comprehend and the smell of Susie's perfume. Nonetheless, I was relieved when Sam decided it was time to move on.

Poverty, I learned first hand, is no damn fun

Mingle With 75,000 Other Car Lovers; Drool Over 9,400 Cool, Customized Old Cars Displayed In A Pastoral 350-Acre Setting. Is This AED Heaven Or What?

It is, indeed, but actually it's Minnesota in the summer. And the Minnesota Street Rod Association simply calls it a "Back To The Fifties" event. Thousands of street rods, customs, classics and restored vehicles, 1964 and older, displayed and cruising the State Fairgrounds.

Four delightful days in June. Days filled with neat cars and neat people making like life was half a century ago. There's even a fifties drive-in, Porky's, offering car-side service "the way it used to be" since it opened for business in 1953.

Minnesotans have only a few weeks for summer fun. Car people make the most of it with events like this. Starting in 1973 with just a few cars and lots of enthusiasm, this car buff gathering has become one of the largest in the world. And it attracts participants from all over the world: England, Europe, Australia, Arab countries…even China.

What does this say about the spread of AED?

He had hired a young street boy, maybe ten or eleven, to watch his Caddy which he had brazenly parked in the "No Parking" zone at the bar's front door. The kid and the Caddy were still there. Sam flipped him a five.

The kid ran off grinning from ear to ear and we were once again on our way in Sam's open air chariot.

"Hell," I thought, "I would have watched his Caddy for five bucks." The Kamstra's lived frugally in those days. Five bucks would have bought new shoes for one of my beautiful daughters back in Duluth.

Five bucks was nothing to Sam. Our next stop was an elegant restaurant, "Chez" something or other. The Maitre d', not surprisingly, knew Sam and we were immediately whisked away to his favorite window table.

"He planned all this when he agreed to be interviewed," I thought. "No damn wonder he was so cordial. Most CEO's hate journalist, won't tell them anything of consequence without a fight. Sam had his own agenda and her name was Susie."

But, what the hell, this was real cost-is-no-object living and I went along with it. The haughty waiter arrived to take our drink order. Without saying a word, he made it clear that my shirtsleeved presence was repugnant to him.

My rum and coke order didn't heighten his esteem.

"Very good, sir." he said, looking down his nose as though I had just made a bad smell.

In this era of my life, I had not yet cultivated a taste for martini's or the single malt Scotch that would one day be a staple in my life. Sam saved the day by ordering his specially prepared dish for all of us: Chateau Briand. I thought it was superb, not that I had any criteria against which to compare it. Bananas Foster, Courvoisier Cognac and coffee capped off the meal. Susie didn't seem overly impressed but I was.

In the day's before single malt scotch

I think I know how Cinderella felt

This was living! One day, I resolved, maitre d's would fawn over me and show me to the best table in the house. I didn't need Susie though. I already had a beautiful wife, a lady who added class as well as stability to my life. I wondered what Sam's wife was like and if she bought his story about this being the night he "had to entertain a magazine writer. "

My part in this charade ended with the elegant dinner. It wasn't yet midnight but I think I know how Cinderella felt. My "pumpkin" would be the grungy commuter train back to my hotel in Washington. Sam dropped me off at the train station, wished me a pleasant trip, then roared off into the night with Susie at his side.

In the years that followed this exotic experience, I would be exposed to all manner of expense accountism. Some of it was essential to starting or strengthening relations with prospects, customers, business associates and others. For the most part, I found myself opting to work extra hours for my clients instead of entertaining them.

My resistance to the never ending lure of the corporate good life was based more on pragmatism than any moral purity. This kind of living makes you feel like you are winning but you really aren't. My ego might be satiated as I sashayed up to Mr. Arrogant Maitre d' and announced "table for Kamstra" but it would still be tuna hot dish next evening at home. My waist line would be growing but not my bank account.

Nothing but money-in-the-bank success was going to satisfy me.

■ ■ ■

Growing my ad agency later, I relied on ideas, service and a genuine interest in clients and their aspirations. Business lunches were just that, business talk. Even if I knew anything about sports, I was more interested in learning everything there was to know about my client. Long nights and weekends were devoted to idea generation, rarely to entertainment.

Entertainment, to be sure, has its place in business relations, but like all pleasurable activities, it can be dangerously addictive.

I recall one particularly pathetic case of such addiction. I'll call him Joe Livinhi although that's obviously not his real name. In his late fifties, he learned that he was about to become a victim of the trend to "corporate downsizing", a euphemism for firing people to bring costs in line. Understandably, Joe was crushed. He had the kind of job people dream about. Through his job, he lived better than most people featured on TV's' "Lives Of The Rich And Famous". His entire career had been dedicated to advance "coordination" of upcoming sales meetings, conventions, incentive travel awards and the like for Worldwide Widgets (not the company name).

Joe had but to invoke the name of Worldwide Widgets and identify himself as meeting coordinator for this mammoth company to get the red carpet treatment anywhere in the world. He was assured the best suite in the house at almost any major hotel or resort.

"Compliments of the house," were the syrupy words that paved the globe trotting pathway of his charmed existence. Breakfast, lunch and dinner were of course on the house too. How else could Joe adequately determine, on behalf of his superiors, that this was indeed an establishment worthy of hosting the annual Worldwide Widgets convention?

Joe's path and mine had crossed occasionally but I couldn't say I knew him well. Our conversations usually concerned some promotional program that my shop was frantically readying for his departure deadline. His demeanor during these exchanges led me to believe that, if he thought about my entrepreneurial existence at all, it was momentary and largely contemptuous. "Vendor" was his favorite term for guys like me.

I, on the other hand, looked at his career path with a certain amount of envy. Grudging, but envy nonetheless. Joe would never find himself peddling artwork on New Year's Eve; especially in a car with a frozen battery.

"Compliments of the house"

Now we would never know

"Maybe," I thought, "I am making all the wrong choices." Later this day – and Joe made me aware of his precise schedule plus the penalties my company would incur for missing any of his deadlines – Joe would be off to sunny Florida. There, he would be playing golf, a game his friends said he had mastered with some skill.

My challenge, on the other hand, would be rescuing my frozen Porsche.

"Take care out there," the bubbly voice of the weather lady came over the radio. "You can freeze to death in a matter of minutes so stay with your car if you have trouble."

I had no intentions of leaving my car, but I had no choice either. In time next day, I rescued my frozen little Porsche and headed back to the warmth of my home.

"You dumb bastard!" I cursed myself as the Porsche chugged and sputtered out of the deserted service station. I envied Joe a whole lot right then.

But now, some years later, Joe was about to lose that cushy job. I wondered as he agonized over his plight if he might have made it on his own. Before he committed his career to the Freebie Train and the momentum became too great for him to get off, was there an embryo entrepreneur or an intrepreneur in him that might have developed?

I would never know. Joe would never know.

Arranging cruises had been one of Joe's specialties. Cruise marketers were especially nice folks.

"Perhaps, Joe…er, Mr. Livinhi, you would like to bring your wife for a get acquainted cruise next month. You know, check out the facilities, the food and the entertainment. After all, as you said, Mr. Livinhi, these are the best of the best Worldwide Widget sales people. We want everything to be just right, do we not?"

"Absolutely," said Joe, and so it went year after year, decade after decade.

Until the downsizing.

Joe didn't see it this way, but he had no discernible talent other than living high in the name of Worldwide Widgets. And now he was being sacked by a merciless management more concerned with profit margins than the mammoth mortgage payments Joe was left to face.

There are probably thousands – more likely hundreds of thousands – of Joe Livinhi's out there, daily inhabiting America's finer restaurants, hotels, resorts and cruise ships. Most will not let the trappings of success trap them into believing, "by God, this is success!" Sadly, many will.

I think about Joe now and then. On occasion, I think of him as my wife and I drift off to sleep in the well appointed stateroom of our sleek cabin cruiser. We never enjoyed a complimentary cruise in our lives. We did, however, thoroughly enjoy writing a check for the full purchase price of our new boat.

■ ■ ■

I think about Joe and I wonder

CHAPTER 21

Race Track Driving;
It Clears The Mind

You really need some hills and a few sharp turns

It Usually comes over you in the more advanced stages of Auto Erotic Dependency (AED). You become overwhelmed by an urge to run with the big boys on a real SCCA-Certified race track. Not necessarily a career change, mind you, but just see what it would be like.

Your AED "speed therapy" so far has never extended beyond blowing the carbon out of a car that has spent too much time in bumper-to-bumper traffic. Carbon elimination begins with the selection of a deserted, hopefully cop-free road; one like you see in those "performance car" commercials. Then you let yourself and your car run free. Go for the big numbers on your odometer and your tach. Straight-a-ways will do the job, but you really need some hills and a few sharp turns to make it fun. Your AED affliction probably needs stick shift treatment, too; a chance to hone your skills in heel-toe-mind coordination.

"How, in the name of all that is holy, could anyone have this kind of fun – or any kind of car fun – without a stick and a clutch? Answer: they couldn't."

Roads with AED therapeutic merit abound in Minnesota as well as its neighboring states. Granted, our fun driving season is pathetically brief but it heightens our appreciation. As I head for my first race track experience, I am winding my way north into the "Lake Country" of Minnesota. Chamber of Commerce types argue that our claim of "10,000 Lakes" is understated, but who wants to quibble? It's just plain beautiful!

Donnybrooke International Speedway, my destination, is a 130-mile drive; longer the way I plot my course. It's a new speedway – opened in 1968 – and nestled on 400-plus acres, overlooking one of Minnesota's 10,000 lakes. Some argue that such a significant speedway should be located in a more populated area. Maybe so, but it is perfect for me.

The willing little four-cylinder engine pushing my 356 Porsche is wound up and so am I. It's under-powered compared to some of the serious "hot shoe" drivers who will join me in the speed events scheduled for the weekend. My "Little Red" is also under-prepared. No special tune-ups. No special tires. Just a wash job and off to the event. Oh yes, and installation of the required fire extinguisher plus the purchase of a helmet meeting racing specs. There will be a safety tech inspection at the track.

Its a hot, mid-summer Friday, 1969. The top is down; my spirits are up. I swing into the parking lot of the headquarters Brainerd motel right after lunch. Porsches and Porsche people are everywhere. My Auto Erotic Gene is becoming over active already.

The entire event has been painstakingly arranged by the Nord Stern Chapter of the Porsche Club of America. One of my first acts, after acquiring my 356, was to join the club. They helped me to realize that I was not alone in my AED affliction; a support group even before support groups had attained political correctness. The club sponsored rallies, tech training, dinners, parties and camaraderie galore. Without the club, I probably never would have tried my hand at race track driving.

Now the time was at hand. After dinner, two hours of class room instruction. Lots of charts and graphs about speed into the turns. Many cautions about the dangers involved and how to prevent injury. Very essential; very hard to keep awake. Our instructor – a bronzed, trim, muscular and stony-faced guy with close-cropped dark hair – was a seasoned race driver with impressive credentials. He left no doubt that he knew what he was talking about and that anyone with any smarts would pay attention.

"If you think racing is all glamour and girls, forget it. It's hard work. It's serious business. People get hurt, barbecued in their cars. People get killed!"

School over, our novice group joined the experienced drivers in the bar. Time for some serious car talk and not-too-serious drinking.

Saturday morning, 6:45 a.m. The cool Northwoods morning was rapidly clearing my head; counteracting the effects of too much bourbon-and-tobacco-laced car talk of the night before. We were gathered in Minnesota's Paul Bunyan Country and had just put away a Bunyan-sized breakfast of steak and eggs. A towering replica of the fabled Bunyan, his mighty woodsman's ax and Babe, his famous Blue Ox, looked down on us as we filed out of the motel and into our Porsches. The sun accentuated the mirror finishes of our beloved cars as we fired them up.

There is no symphony on earth quite as soul-stirring as an acre of Porsche engines all cackling, rumbling and roaring to life in unison.

"People get killed!"

> *"Let's brake too soon! Let's brake too soon!"*

We filed out of the parking lot and onto the highway for the 6 mile run from Brainerd to the Donnybrooke Speedway. I caught myself fantasizing about burning up the track in my little red machine. This morning, the novice drivers would walk the track while the experienced drivers readied their machines for the coming speed events. Our instructor would "walk us through" the ten turns, the straights and general layout of the 3-mile track.

I learned that, at this juncture in America's growing love affair with auto racing, Donnybrooke had the distinction of being the fastest of them all. It was built for speeds of 200 miles per hour on the straights. That was twice the speed capability of my Porsche and considerably beyond any speed I would be considering at this stage in my racing "career".

As we walked and learned, our instructor let us in on the secret of how professional drivers "straighten" the turns to gain a few seconds of better timing. These drivers find the optimum "line" through the turn, "fudging" on the track's actual configuration by running slightly onto the grass. Doing so with the utmost caution. The "line" strategy raises hell with tires and suspensions; and could trigger a spin out.

Training to qualify for driving on the track is brief but intense: class room, walk-the-track; then a qualified driver takes you through the course "at speed." That's the scary part. My assigned trainer is Randall, younger than my "late thirties" by a decade. Participating in two wars has, once again, put me way behind schedule. As we start the training drive, I think Randall's name might better be "Rambo". He is fearless. We blast onto the track and down the first 3/4 mile straight. Rambo's voice cuts through the noise of his 911 Porsche as we approach turn one. I would estimate our speed at 120 or better.

"It's all in knowing just when to brake. Not too soon. Not too late," he says. There's a matter-of-factness in voice that only intensifies my terror. We are only scant yards from the turn and Rambo shows no sign of braking.

"Let's brake too soon! Let's brake too soon!" I want to plead with him. But I don't. I sit in stoic silence, hiding my terror as best I can. Now I know how Mimi must feel having to put her faith and her life in my fast-driving judgment. I couldn't do it. I could never be comfortable trusting my life to someone else's driving, no matter how skilled.

Finally – just when I am sure Rambo has pushed his luck too far and it's all over for us – he brakes. But only for a few seconds and then he is "standing on it" again.

"Don't lose your speed", Rambo yells. You should hit the gas right after you brake. Come out of the turn at full throttle."

"Good God!", I think, "we've got nine more turns to go. If I live through this, maybe I should just take my graduation certificate and go home. I can always hang it on my den wall and make up hero stories."

We make it to the finish line. I scamper out of Rambo's 911 and head for a hamburger.

"How'd it go?", my fellow novices ask.

"Great!", I lie. "Really a ball."

After lunch, we gather at the pit area for a drivers meeting. I feel more like I belong. One of the boys. Our team leader repeats the safety precautions one more time. Then he goes over the rules of the game.

"This is an auto cross event; not a race. You will be timed from the tower. Your competition is yourself and how much you know about taking that Porsche of yours through its paces. Don't take on the guy on the track next to you. Give him space. Give him courtesy. Okay, when your car is ready, line up by the numbers. You'll be flagged onto the track starting at 1:30."

*"Great!" I lie.
"Really a ball"*

"What am I doing here?"

My number is 11. Just happenstance, but an easy number to create with masking tape applied to the doors. The seasoned drivers had nicely crafted, "store bought" numbers. Many brought their fully-prepared, fully-groomed machines on flat beds or enclosed trailers. Some included extra sets of tires; tires that would give the driver the best traction depending on weather conditions. I was more curious than jealous.

Maybe I would someday get really, "equipment serious" about competitive driving, but it was unlikely. My philosophy has always been to bring my Porsche – and other cars to come – into every day, workaday life. No pedestals, no pampering. Have fun at family events or driving to work. Enjoy calling on clients; especially out of town, out of state clients.

Time to line up for my first run. Donnybrooke has parking space for 30,000 cars and seating, picnicking space for spectators. There are few spectators for this Porsche Club event; wives, friends, family, a few local auto buffs is it. Nonetheless I can understand the "on stage" appeal to those truly into race track driving. You could start thinking of yourself as a gladiator and hope that comely young chicks in the audience see you in the same light. My thinking can be summed up in just five words:

"What am I doing here?"

I'm buckled in, helmeted, racing the engine to signify that I'm ready to roll. Then I'm flagged onto the track. I floor it as I head down the straight. Little Red climbs up to the 100 mph mark but that is about all its 60 horsepower can do. Trans-Am Champion Mark Donohue recommends at least 150 mph on this strait and something close to 140 into the turn. This is a track where raw horsepower and raw courage have the advantage. I am somewhat short on both. Like my instructor, Rambo, Donohue cautions against losing speed on this first turn.

Auto cross events require placement of pylons at turn one. I suspect it is to discourage show offs from hurting themselves or wrecking their cars at this high speed turn. Each driver must zig zag through the route of the pylons. Knock one over and you lose points as well as face. The pylons, of course, multiply the difficulty of maintaining speed.

"Enough"

I found myself bearing down on turn one with good speed; then made the mistake of braking early. You can't recover from this dumb mistake. Shift down. Slam down the accelerator. Swear your head off. You will never regain your first-straight momentum once you've lost it. Turn two is recommended at 120 mph. Yeah, right. I try to remember the "line" we were taught but decide against the risk of rolling Little Red and breaking my neck in the process. No roll bar. Many drivers "lose it" on turn two. During warm up runs, one of the experienced members did an end-over-end flip that totaled his 911 but only scratched the driver. I tried not to think about it.

Most people go through life thinking they know all about fast driving. They believe that if Smokey would just get off their back they could easily out-drive their fellow motorists. A few minutes on a race track will prove otherwise. Except for the pros who work at – make a career of it – most of us would just get in the way of those who really know about driving flat out on a race track.

In the years that followed my unspectacular racing debut, I improved my track time. Did it with more Donnybrook runs and a bigger, faster 911. I even tried running on State Fair Grounds ovals. Boring!

Then I decided. Enough. A life broadening experience that I would not have wanted to miss. I would always wish I had at least tried. Now I can embellish the tale of my track accomplishments as I retell it to my grandchildren. I tried it. It was fun. It was enough.

Racing. It clears the mind.

■ ■ ■

CHAPTER 22

Your Car: More Sinned Against Than Sinner

Mother Nature consumes us all

It's spring in Minnesota. My Mercedes and I – each of us aging somewhat gracefully – are about to engage in a Minnesota spring ritual: coming out of hibernation. Even more than usual, it has "been a long winter". Temperatures have plunged to 50 below; wind chills to 80 below and worse. Assuming you get your car started, it's pure hell – if you can imagine hell at 50 below – to drive. Everything squeaks and groans. Tires seem to have been frozen into square blocks. Exhaust from other vehicles, rises in billows to obscure your vision.

"Do not leave your car if you have trouble; exposed skin will freeze in a matter of seconds." With more than 100 inches of snow, who would be dumb enough to wander off anyway? Then, again, we are dumb enough to live here, aren't we? It does keep out the riff raff, I keep telling myself.

Minnesotans are aware that if you hit another car, both will shatter into a million pieces; and the pieces probably just swept away by the street department. The ever-vigilant road crews have been dumping salt – three tons per every ton of snowfall – since the first snow in October.

"The Upper Midwest", as we like to call this country, is not car lovers' country. If you want to protect your car, you store it and drive a "winter beater" until spring finally comes. The beater will one day disintegrate into a fine rusty powder, but your "good car" will be safe. More or less.

Lest you feel smug because you live in California or some other car-friendly climate; your car, too, is slowly being destroyed by nature. In Minnesota, we just accelerate the process with salt.

In one of the more obscene acts of demagogic gall, Al Gore has made himself rich and – more or less – famous by "defending" Mother Nature against the onslaught of automobiles. In truth, it is your car that needs defending from the vengeful forces of Mother Nature. The old girl can take care of herself just fine without environmental Doom Squads; thank you. Patiently, relentlessly, she will ultimately consume all our cars; and Al Gore too for that matter.

Leave your car outside and exposed to the environment long enough and you will return to a rusting, rotting pile of junk. This is a theoretical experiment and one you cannot try at home, of course. To begin with, you need your car.

What's more, if you left your car – almost anywhere in the world – it would be stolen long before your environmental experiment could ever be validated.

You, however, are an AED person; you are not interested in any damn fool experiments to watch your car disintegrate. You want to keep your car; fondle it, fuss over it. You are not unaware that cars these days cost more than houses once did. It's more than "okay to love your car"; it's financially shrewd and absolutely essential if you would delay nature's defiling and ultimate decomposition of your beloved car. The Auto Immune could care less, but this is a book for car lovers.

Showroom new after 30 years

Take it from one who nurtures his cars for decades, not years; you can defend against Mother Nature's wrath, but in time, you loose. Cars don't really wear out or die of old age; they die for want of protective, loving care. My car "collection", for instance, began innocently and unintentionally in the late l960's. As a car buff with a hyper active Auto Erotic Gene, I just couldn't part with my pristine "old model" at trade-in time. And so it has transpired through the seventies, the eighties and into the new century; each old car has been "kept in the family"; saved over the futile protests of my Auto Immune, but lovingly tolerant, wife.

One car in this unintentional collection is a 1969 Mercedes 280SE sedan. Purchased new, with special paint, white leather, "the works"– the full price just $8,400. It still looked showroom new when the dealer offered a generous $1,200 trade-in in the mid seventies. It still looks showroom new as I continue to drive it – and admire it – more than 30 years later. The classic (to me) old Mercedes is probably worth a bit more than its l969 new car price; but that's not why I keep it. It's a beautiful – almost regal – solid machine. As road worthy as the days when – as a family – we joyfully toured America coast-to-coast. This old Mercedes has character; even soul. There's not much of that to be found in today's automobiles. Most important, this car belongs in the Kamstra family.

Precision bombings

And today's the day the Mercedes and I relive our youth as we head for the Minnesota countryside, which is also awakening from its long winter slumber. Road crews have replaced salt with millions of gallons of gooey black tar; they dump it on road surfaces, adding gravel on top. Guess who gets to mix this mess and pound it into the road bed. You do.

I head for a side road, but not before the pristine Mercedes picks up several pounds of the insidious tar-gravel mixture. It will be enough to keep me busy with tar removal until, say, July.

Saving your car from its natural enemies – not to mention road crews and the hordes of environmental crazies who hate all cars – will never be easy. The attack of Mother Nature's "take-no-prisoners" forces begins even before you take possession of your car. As you proudly drive it home; for every ounce of the much maligned exhaust coming from your car, Mom Nature has cooked up tons of her own special crud recipe to honor the occasion.

Consider her multi-billion-bird air force, for instance. Birds have a built in navigation system and "smart bomb" capability that puts any modern day air force to shame. Their preferred target is a just-polished or just-purchased car; bombs away at the exact moment the proud owner has stepped back to admire his or her shiny set of wheels. This kind of precision bombing is repeated billions of times every hour of every day in every corner of the globe. Bird droppings don't concern the Auto Immune motorists, of course, unless the offending feces should land directly on their heads. Those of us who lavish love on our cars, however, should be worried.

It's more serious than just the affront represented by fresh bird poop on the mirror finish of your car.

The stuff is composed of acids fully capable of eating through battleship armor. Its formulation is a manifestation of a basic rule of nature: "Everything In Nature Devours Everything Else In Nature".

Thus, even a bird's '"stool" – to use the precise medical term – must perpetuate this age old natural phenomenon. Neglect to immediately wash off bird poop and your car may forever show the scars of your neglect. The etching-through-polish-paint-and-steel begins before the offensive fecal matter has even dried. There are ways to fight back – all of them imperfect – which we shall discuss.

As an emergency measure, I once used a dab of my very best bourbon – kept in the trunk in case of snake bite – to dab away at fresh bird gunk.

As we now know, everything in nature is busy devouring everything else in nature. Birds obey this natural law by eating yucky, squishy bugs. It is a widely held belief in scientific circles that this diet has much to do with the corrosive power of bird poop. Bug innards, as any of us who have driven through the countryside on a summer's day know, deposits itself directly on every exterior surface of your car. Bugs carry on this mindless, suicide bomber attack without benefit of first making their way through the digestive system of birds. This direct assault multiplies the paint-etching potential of bug intestines.

As a child, you may remember asking your parents, "why did God make bugs?" Now you know.

While we are considering assaults from the heavens, consider rain. As the old 280 and I are tooling along the back roads, an unexpected – and damn well unpredicted – shower happens. Watching the rain drops bounce off the freshly waxed hood of the Mercedes I could easily be lulled into thinking of it as a benign blessing of nature. Maybe it will even wash away some grit and salt from the road. Yes, but.

Think again. Each innocent little drop of rain is probably a "carrier". It brings to any car's finish all kinds of microscopic-sized airborne gunk; gritty, shitty gunk that is anything but friendly to your car; car hungry gunk. "Acid rain" is the popular term. "Acid" is the operative word. Rain is nature's way of saying "I'm going to feast on your car."

"Why did God make bugs?"

Nature will prevail

Several layers of polish, preservative and wax help the Mercedes fight off this latest attack. This old car has withstood many an assault from Mother Nature and her allies since l969. Still, I'll be sure to wash it as soon as we get home.

Then, as suddenly as it began, the shower ends. One of the little extra pleasures of sitting at the controls of an aging Mercedes is watching the sun glint off the famous three-pointed star. That's where the star should be; right up there front and center where the owner can watch the sun reflect its glory. Newer Mercedes models insert the star into the front grill; like a giant belly button. Wind tunnel smart, but not the same. As more sun streams into the Mercedes, I am warmed by the real wood trim everywhere; even around the windows. I bask in the thought of the craftsmanship that must have gone into the selection, cutting and fitting of the wood trim. Best of all, these craftsmen – probably all retired now – had the good sense to leave the wood looking and feeling like wood. Before they retired, I wish they would have passed along their trade secrets to the present generation of Mercedes wood craftsmen.

"Hey, guys, don't polish that beautiful walnut till it looks like plastic, for God's sake!"

Enough basking in my sun-drenched, made-by-guys-who-cared Mercedes. Mother Nature is attacking again! This time the attack comes from millions of miles out in space. Friendly old Sol is not at all friendly to aging old German cars or aging old drivers either, for that matter. Blazing, baking sun takes away the youthful luster of your skin; it does the same to your car's skin.

Rain drops bead up on the majestic hood of the 280SE. The beads confirm the thoroughness of my most recent and loving wax job. I don't kid myself. Each drop serves as a magnifier for the sun's rays. Mother Nature has a counter measure for each and every protective strategy we car lovers attempt.

Nature will prevail.

A breeze as gentle as the rain dries the Mercedes; but not before it has deposited some of its billions of particles of impurities: chemicals, paint spray, salt and who knows what. Your car: more sinned against than sinner.

Some of us can, of course, hide our cars in our garages during inclement weather. For a disproportionately large part of my life, I could not afford this luxury. Some very fine cars disintegrated as a result. Hiding you car in the garage will, of course, deny you not only the fun of year around motoring but of knowing that – on any given day – envious neighbors will be eating their little hearts out as they gaze wistfully upon that special vehicle of yours as it sits arrogantly in your drive..

Not incidentally, if you have a tree-lined drive, maybe you should forget leaving the car out for show. Trees usually have birds. Birds have notoriously inconsiderate bowel habits. Well, you know all about that. But trees pelt your pet car with resins and sap that are next to impossible to remove.

Inside your garage, however, you will only slow – not stop – nature's relentless campaign to eat your car.

Some wiseacre car cynic once said that if you turned off the lights in your garage and stood very silently, you could actually hear your Porsche rusting. This is true. Rust is nature's most lethal weapon for decomposing all metal in the universe. Why God chose to concentrate specially on Porsches may never be known. Maybe he had a bad experience with one. My first Porsche mostly dissolved before my eyes…and before I learned to take better care of my cars.

In my defense, I must reiterate that I live in Minnesota where salt tonnage dumped on streets and highways exceeds the annual snow fall. It is said that *Bad Barf*, the salt Cargoyle (see next page), prefers this state over all others. In fairness to Porsche, it must be noted that Porsche and most all cars have made great strides in rust-retarding finishes in the last 20 years. Nonetheless, my old Porsche comes out of hibernation only in late spring and only after several rainfalls have washed away the banks of salt left behind by zealous highway crews.

Rust is only one of Mother Nature's in-your-face-in-your-garage confrontations. A well known auto journalist, for instance, found that one of natures lovable critters – a raccoon – had eaten a good share of his Ferrari's interior leather. It happened while the Ferrari was "safely" in the family garage awaiting his

"Bad Barf", the salt Cargoyle, prefers Minnesota over all other states

Bad Barf

Bad Barf moseyed into town some decades ago. Boys over at the Highway Department invited him; said he would help folks get around in nasty weather. A ton of salt here, a ton of salt there and first thing you know, old Barf has made all that ice and snow go away. What the boys really don't like to talk about is that old Barf is darn well getting rid of our cars in the process. The stuff he spews just plain eats cars, roads, plants and what all. Costs a few billion every year to replace all those cars, roads and things; but, what the hell, old Barf is just doin' his job. Barf's melt-away-rust-away methods have been obsolete for years; better chemicals, less cost. Trouble is, nobody dares bring it up to Bad Barf. They say old Cargoyles never die. Shucks, they don't even fade away.

■ ■ ■

Barf spots you there
in snow or ice.
"I'll spew some salt;
won't that be nice?"

Nice? Get real!
Old Barf's a beast.
Your car, once salted,
becomes his feast.

return. Mice, rats and other creatures consider garaged cars a gourmet treat, too; and they don't insist on Ferrari's with fine Connelly leather either. Upholstery and carpets are preferred as a entrees with, perhaps, a little wiring insulation for dessert.

"Keep it clean"

Moisture translates into rust; it also means mildew can happen. When it does, the stink may well stay with your car through all eternity. As this is being written, my favorite source of storage protection products and advice is a little company called B.W. Incorporated in Browns Valley, Minnesota. Good Minnesota folks with a damn good business idea.

Inside your car's engine is no safe haven from Mom Nature either. Lubricants decompose, become acidic and attack your fine engine even when you haven't gone near the car since the last oil change. My rites-of-spring procedure for the old Mercedes always includes fresh oil. Then I drive for miles trying to find a station that still sells genuine, undiluted gasoline.

A new attack on the big, old, fuel-injected Mercedes straight six is "gas" made from corn. Crazed ecologists have conspired with farm lobbies to ordain that the damn stuff be used in all cars. What this stuff might do to your car's engine – or your boat or whatever – be damned. It is now the politically correct thing to do to "save the planet."

When Mother Nature teams up with ecologists, farmers, big business corn processors and politicians, there probably is no defense for the poor car freak. There are some things you can do to protect your car from other natural and unnatural attacks, however. This book will not attempt to play a "How To" role in protecting your beloved machine. It will point you in the right direction and you take it from there.

My first rule is "keep it clean". You can't wash a car too often even if your Auto Immune neighbors and friends ridicule and revile you as "obsessive compulsive." You know in your heart that it is okay to love your car. What better way to show it than to shower it with love – along with soap and water. I like Ivory Liquid; the same stuff your wife – or you – use for dishes. You can use another household product if you prefer or you can go out and spend much more money for "specially compounded" car washing solutions. Some fanatics urge you to put a little corn oil (better in the water than in the gas) to restore oils you may be washing from the paint.

The thing is to do it yourself. This is not a matter of proving that you are indeed blessed with the Auto Erotic Gene. It is common sense. Have you taken a close look at the sullen creatures who man car washes these days? Can you imagine they have anything but contempt for people who care about their cars? Have you looked at those whirling brushes that would defile your cars finish? Car washes were invented for Philistines and the Auto Immune who mostly lease their cars anyway.

Never ever give in to appeals from the Girl Scouts, Boy Scouts, Lutherans For Abstinence or any other group wanting to wash your car as a fund raiser. Just give them the cash – if their cause seems just – and then drive away as fast as you can. You will never again be able to love your car after a horde of youngsters have been over it with sand-laden home sponges and water that hasn't been changed since yesterday.

When you have gently and lovingly washed your own car you will be faced with new dilemmas at drying time:

    a. Is a chamois best and should it be genuine or simulated?

    b. Are towels better and can you get by with using bathroom towels?

    c. Is it true that used – but clean – diapers are best for both washing, drying and later polishing?

I prefer "c" but you can't get into too much trouble with any of the above. Again, the important thing is to keep ahead of Mother Nature and her allies; washing off the crud as fast as it lands on your car.

Even a lovingly washed car is not necessarily clean, however. Your car's paint dies a little every day from a combination of "natural causes". You may have picked up road tar, tree sap and who knows what. It all has to come off – along with the dead paint – until you get down to the original "live" paint.

Lutherans for Abstinence

Cliff Helling On Family, AED Genes...And '34 Fords: "The Lines are Right"

Visit Cliff Helling's 1934 Ford-packed restoration shop if you want to step back 60-plus years into automotive history. He will wax eloquent about the perfect lines of this particular Ford. You will also learn about his family "lines" that carry unmistakable evidence of early AED genes.

Cliff's dad, Cliff Helling, Sr., entrepreneur and Barney Oldfield racing buddy, was a classic example of a man afflicted with the AED gene.

This 1934 Ford Phaeton, a 4-door convertible restored by Cliff, has the "lines" he loves to admire.

"He wasn't afflicted with the gene, he was endowed with it," Cliff, Jr. insists. "He even convinced Barney to sell him his beloved Stutz Bearcat. Used it to impress my mom when they were dating. Showing off what alcohol injection – in the motor, not the driver – will do to increase speed, he blew one engine head right through the hood. Stutz had wooden hoods back in those days".

Cliff, born (1935) of the marriage that followed the Stutz Bearcat dating, inherited a full measure of the AED gene. He owned, raced, and often wrecked more than 100 cars – mostly '33 and '34 Fords – before his 18th birthday. That's when Uncle Sam had him driving tanks during the Korean War.

Retired from his education career now, he concentrates on restoring and enjoying his favorite 1934 Fords. They include the exquisite Phaeton, three and five-window coupes – many with rumble seats – and even a "Ute", a car/truck combination 60 years ahead of today's SUV's. "Just for the hell of it" Cliff even installed a Ford flathead V8 in his '52 9N Ford tractor. "Road Speed!" My brother, Lewis, would have been jealous. Cliff's favorite '34 Ford "Woody" has seen more than 50,000 miles of Helling touring.

I knew why the '34 Ford held fond memories for me (my first car), but I asked Cliff why he singled out this model over all other cars.

"I love 'em! They're fast. They're beautiful. The eye flows over those wonderful, Edsel Ford-inspired lines and there is a satisfaction to the viewer that says 'this is right'".

The author and Cliff Helling pose by one of Cliff's '34 Fords. Ken Kamstra's first car; Cliff's every day AED therapy car.

What kind of compounds, cleaners, polishes, etc. – and how they should be applied – is the subject for an entire book; certainly not this one. Not every car buff has the skill, the temperament or even the right tools to "detail" a car to concours standards. There are as many theories, articles and opinions on the subject as there are products that claim to do it best. For starters, I recommend a book by James Joseph entitled *Auto Detailing The Professional Way*.

The mirror finish of a properly cleaned-polished-preserved-waxed finish is a thing of awe and beauty to behold. It is "applied" auto love at its finest. Learn the art or hire it done. It will multiply and perpetuate the pleasure of your love relationship with your car.

You can defend you car against the assaults of Mother Nature and those who would pretend to defend the planet from your car. Al Gore can't help being dull; your car can.

Applied Auto Love

■ ■ ■

Cliff Helling, Sr. shows off the now legendary Stutz Bearcat that he acquired from his friend, the famous Barney Oldfield.

Cliff and one of his '34 Fords; reading his favorite book, a Ford manual.

CHAPTER 23

THE INVASION OF THE CARGOYLES; HOW IT ALL BEGAN

"Aaaroogle. Aaaroogle"

It's midnight in Washington, January 2, 1974. President Richard Nixon and First Lady, Pat Nixon, are trying to get some sleep. At least, they tell themselves, it is the new year, and Mr. Nixon feels certain that, whatever happens, it couldn't be worse than 1973. That "damned Watergate thing" was starting to close in on him. An achiever himself – and an ardent football fan – Nixon sometimes envies guys like O.J. Simpson whose careers are always on the rise and trouble free. Just last year, O.J. set another record, rushing more than 2,000 yards in one year.

"Damn it all! O.J. sets speed records, and I have to order everyone to slow down" Nixon mumbles as he tries still another pillow position; hoping desperately that it might bring blessed sleep. "Fifty five miles an hour – Christ!"

"What, dear?"

"Nothing."

Some time later, muted snoring is heard coming from the presidential bedroom. It is the only sound in an atmosphere of almost unearthly silence throughout the White House. Bright – but yet foreboding – moonlight sends shafts of light helter skelter into the magnificent presidential quarters. Trees swaying in the wind outside, intermittently disrupt the light shafts, making them dance to a soundless choreography. Weird!

The evil new law – the Emergency Highway Energy Conservation Act– lay on the president's desk in the oval office. One of the dancing moon beams finds its target: the history-making document lying just next to the pen that was used to consummate this heinous act.

The intermittent light shafts continue to stab at the document as if in an effort to energize it; to give it life. It responds! At first it is an almost imperceptible movement. More stabs of moonlight. There is now a rhythmic pulsating. Could this be the way Frankenstein was born?

Then sounds break the silence.

"Aaaroogle. Aaaroogle." It is a gurgling sound followed by labored breathing.

A grotesque metamorphosis is taking place right in the Oval Office; this hallowed place where so much history had already happened; the nerve center of the free world. Now it is being defiled by the birth of this thing; this frightening creature.

Flesh, some kind of flesh, was forming. Light shafts – still performing their pagan dance atop the president's desk – seemed to accelerate the transmutation that was now clearly underway. The flesh glistened; seemed to welcome the moonlight playing over its body. A head was forming; its eyes bulged. The mouth taking shape was gaping and out of all proportion to the body. Its expression was at once fierce and friendly. Inscrutable, it defied mortal description.

That was it – immortal! Students of medieval history would surely have noted its resemblance to the gargoyles of centuries past. This creature, however, was of the genus "Cargoyle®"; of the Gargoyle family but distinguished by its congenital hatred of cars and things mechanical. Like Gargoyles, "Cargoyles" are, indeed, immortal, living on and on through the centuries. This "Cargoyle" would come to be known – not lovingly – by the nickname, "Gotcha", since his sole purpose in life was to capture, humiliate and rob humans traveling more than 55 miles per hour.

■ ■ ■

Flesh, some kind of flesh, was forming

® Cargoyle is a registered trademrk of Ken Kamstra.

Gotcha

The most feared and furtive of all Cargoyles, Gotcha is everywhere and he is nowhere. Chameleon-like, he may appear as a billboard. a clump of bushes, a field of corn, or, perhaps, that pokey, pukey colored sedan you just blew by. Gotcha may even be watching you from the sky. Meet him face to face and you are not likely to forget the experience. His Gotcha glare turns even the most macho lead foot into a sniveling, groveling, lying wimp. You hope that your degrading display of humility and remorse will be rewarded with a reduced fine or maybe just a slap-on-the-wrist warning. It won't. Gotcha has his orders. From his birthplace in Washington and on down to each state legislature, they are clear and straightforward: "Take no crap from these low life evil-doers; just take their money!" ▪ Surrender your money when Gotcha's got you dead to rights. Admit that driving fast is a national disgrace. Give money but don't give up the fun of driving.

■ ■ ■

He waits for you,
the "Gotcha" guy.
behind a bush
or in the sky.

If you get caught,
don't beg or plead.
Just pay your fine
and then proceed.

America got the message

Congressmen, not surprisingly, wasted little time in denying reality; giving the event the proper "spin". They assured their constituents that the monstrous National Maximum Speed Limit (NMSL) would be with us a very short while.

"We ask each and every American to do his or her part during this oil crisis," said the congressional spokesman, referring to the threatened Arab oil embargo on shipments to the U. S. "Therefore, we have passed temporary emergency legislation – and I emphasize temporary – forbidding any citizen to exceed 55 miles per hour while operating a motor vehicle upon any public roadway in this great nation of ours." It was an impassioned speech. "These acts of patriotism, from which I am sure no good American will shrink, will save our precious fuel and keep this great nation rolling during these trying times."

The spokesman droned on, but America got the message.

"Slow your driving to a crawl or we will arrest you and take large sums of cash from you. We might even take away your driving license."

It had happened. America was now under "uniform" speed laws. Most motorists, because they wanted to be good citizens and because they believed the sacrifice would be only a "temporary" inconvenience, were willing to comply.

In capitol halls right after the announcement, congressmen good naturedly chastised each other. No, they weren't concerned that there was no good evidence that poky driving would save much fuel; it was that, in the heat of the debate, they had forgotten the cardinal rule of congressional action: "It's not necessary that you actually do something so long as you appear to be doing something."

And so it was that America became a nation under totalitarian speed control.

The "Gotcha Cargoyle" was loose in the land, multiplying. His every utterance was law. Docile American motorists – more than 150 million of them – were not only brought to a crawl but brought to their knees as well. From their kneeling position, they begged the "Gotcha" enforcers for forgiveness and, if not forgiveness, at least a lesser fine.

"Please," they would plead, "I didn't realize I was going over 55."

Their shameless whining fell on deaf ears. What they didn't realize was that fines were the life blood of the "Gotcha" game. Grudgingly, one had to admire the simple genius of the game: you disobey, you pay. It was an extortion scheme that almost anyone could play. It would work for every state, county, municipality, hamlet or other enforcement authority in the land.

To be sure, the "Gotcha" was making enemies with all his arresting and fine-collecting, but he had friends where it counted. New government bureaus were created or enlarged along with thousands of new government careers. Millions – hundreds of millions – in tax dollars were collected to fund the "Gotcha's" work. The irony of it all, was that the very people being harassed and arrested were having their paychecks further shrunk to pay for the burgeoning "Gotcha" forces. Our tax dollars at work.

Congress had no worries about a motorist revolt; apathetic drivers seemed forever destined to be unorganized and voiceless in capitol corridors. The "Gotcha" regulations were, in fact, soon enhanced with a unique numbers game. In it, each speeding ticket added points to the "sin score" of the offending driver. The points, in turn, increased the fines and could ultimately revoke the sinner's right to drive at all.

Like flies to honey, insurance companies saw the point system as a way to extract even more money – higher premiums – from those "dangerous" drivers who exceeded 55 mile speed limits.

The "Gotcha" Gargoyle was networking; ever increasing his circle of friends and supporters. Anyone attempting to end or threaten his rein of terror would first have to deal with all the powerful people who had reason to love him.

Liberals, for instance, convinced that every citizen needed their enlightened help in all facets of daily life, loved the "Gotcha" most of all. To them, he was one of their crowning achievements: absolute power over the driving conduct of every American able to operate a motor vehicle.

> *An extortion scheme that almost anyone could play*

Bigger and even more evil Cargoyle mutations

To the dismay of those who enjoy driving – and to the AED-addicted who must drive to survive – the Auto Immune politicians happily extended the "Gotcha's " rein to 1975, 1976, 1977, 1978, 1979, 1980…and on and on, decade after decade. As the year 2,000 approached, states were grudgingly given latitude to reconsider the idiotic 55 mph speed limits. Some, like my ultra liberal home state of Minnesota, would fight on to save the "Gotcha" and keep its citizens creeping along forever.

In time, agonizing time, break neck speeds of 65 were permitted on some roads; but not without warnings that highway slaughter would most certainly result.

In l996, Ralph Nader's presidential candidacy would heap scorn on those who dared threaten "Gotcha's" rein. Nader – pompous puppet of the trial lawyers' lobby and lifelong foe of the auto – surprised almost no one with his "keep-them-crawling" position. A liberal's liberal, he and his "Green Party" would forever protect us from our evil driving instincts and/or our tendency to be unkind to animals and trees.

As the creep-vs-cruise battle lines form across the U.S., The "Gotcha" Cargoyle has little to fear. Immortality is his. He has already terrorized a nation; humbling and impoverishing its citizens for more than two decades. He has launched the ubiquitous "Cargoyle" conspiracy. "Gotcha" now has siblings, family. The Big Brother Hatcheries have bred bigger and even more evil "Cargoyle" mutations.

As the Cargoyle conspiracy was taking root, Nixon's Watergate problems eventually did him in; and even O.J. couldn't keep his career star rising indefinitely. Auto enthusiasts, on the other hand, would be plagued by "Cargoyles" into eternity.

■ ■ ■

The Treasure Hunt That Never Ends

A beautifully restored 1930 Cadillac Phaeton, John Kinkead's latest prize. Just listening to its 16-cylinder engine is instant AED therapy.

John Kinkead has been on an automotive treasure hunt most of his adult life. Not the least of his rewards is ongoing AED therapy. If there is a downside to his pursuit, it is that ultimately he must keep selling his treasures to fund another find. Another restoration challenge.

Bringing a 70 or 80 year old car from the brink of extinction is a daunting task. It can take years; sometimes as much as 20 years. And more patience than most people possess. Then one day it is finished.

"It's impossible to put into words the feeling that comes over you when you hit the starter and the car comes to life. Classics are often as massive in size as they are magnificent to behold. You sight down the length of the hood and see gleaming metal, chrome… character. The car has regained its youth and, for the moment at least, so have you."

John's first "resurrection" challenge, more than 50 years ago was a rare 1931 Model A 400. Since then he has restored more than 15 classics. Among the more memorable ones: a 1940 Packard Darrin and a 1930 Rolls Royce Town Car. The Town Car had started life as a sedan, then was converted to a hearse. John, uncompromising in his restoration standards, restored the Rolls Royce to its original proud status as a luxury Town Car.

What happens when they are restored?

"I don't sell them; they are bought," says John. He means that classic car affectionados hear about them and seek him out. Money in hand. Cash from these sales underwrites the next stage of Kinkead's perpetual treasure hunt.

All AED addicts everywhere are enriched by John Kinkead's efforts and those of thousands of other classic car buffs who perpetuate the heritage represented by the "Golden Age" of automotive history.

CHAPTER 24

THE GREAT SILVER BIMMER VS THE "GOTCHA CARGOYLE"

April, 1974. The omnipresent and omnipotent "Gotcha" Cargoyle is now loose in our land, transforming it backward into history – Poke-along Territory.

Or so he thinks.

The new car fix

I'm in our land, too, and about to perform one of the most joyous rituals of AED auto addiction: the new car fix. In most social situations, we are hopeless, hapless misfits. At cocktail parties, we try to talk cars to people whose eyes glaze over as though we were trying to explain the theory of relativity. We don't dare park where normal people park. We spend our Saturdays tinkering with our cars while our neighbors head for the golf course. We take back roads while others relish the efficient boredom of the freeway.

But we have it all over the Auto Immune when it comes to the car buying ritual. To the Auto Immune, car buying is more routine than ritual: take in present car; get taken by car dealer; take home new model; get on with life.

What these deprived people cannot grasp is that choosing and buying a car is an art form. You must savor each step in the process even as you deal with unsavory people with whom you must do business.

In my impoverished days – a seemingly endless era of my early life – I worked part time in a gas station. We called them gas stations in those days. The job paid me – more or less – to tinker with cars. It was also an opportunity to scope out my next used car purchase. One was a big hulking, l2-cylinder Lincoln Zephyr, vintage l939. A local preacher drove it and I saw to it that it got regular washing, lubrication and the like. Every few months, I would ask him:

"Are you about ready to sell this car?"

"Nope, son," he would say, "but I'll sure let you know when I'm ready".

One day he was ready and I rushed right down to the bank to close the deal and start making payments. It was a magnificent machine to behold. Better to behold than to actually drive as it turned out. Its thirst for gas was exceeded only by its thirst for oil. Seems the kindly old reverend had been adding one hell of a lot of oil between changes; probably bought it by the case. He was a bit more experienced at the car buying/selling game than I was.

To keep the Lincoln, I would have been locked in poverty forever.

■ ■ ■

I thought about that old Lincoln and about my extended poverty, years later, as my plane neared Chicago. There are far more opportunities in America than there are people willing to take on the challenge; that, I said to myself, is what makes this such a great country. I'll never be sure about the hereafter, but I know it's not the place to discover that you might have made something more of your life if only you had stopped whining and blaming others.

Here I was about to rub elbows with Ferrari and BMW buyers. Ken Kamstra, the high school drop out; last of the litter of 13 "underprivileged" South Dakota farm kids. Ken Kamstra, former plumber's assistant, painter, laborer, merchant marine sailor and general underachiever. Failure. Failure only toughens the resolve of the determined. I was determined. I found – and some

> "Car buying should be an adventure, an event"

times fought – my way out of poverty; and now a Ferrari salesman would be meeting my flight. I wouldn't be buying a car to affirm my success; this journey was the culmination of a very specific car search. I had been researching the evolution of BMW's 3.0 CS Coupe and I wanted one before they halted production. Automotive editors couldn't praise it enough. *Road & Track* called its engine "the most sophisticated in-line six in the world". They described its body style as "crisp, aggressive and functional without straining to be swoopy."

I lusted for its body, too. It has the makings of a classic, I thought, and, besides, I need that cavernous trunk to carry the "pizza cases" that daily contain the idea gems of my agency.

The salesman met my flight as promised and we were off to the dealership. The AED genes within my body were becoming hyper active. They made it hard for me to suppress a joyful shout as we pulled up to the showroom on Chicago's north side. We were going to have fun this day, but I had to keep my cool; keep the selling price down.

Dreams cost less in 1974. The BMW of my dreams was $13,400 with air, leather, sun roof – the works. A new Ferrari Dino was just under $16,000. Of course, six figure incomes were rare then; in fact – not many years before this milestone event – the more successful Madison Avenue admen were "$10,000-a-year-men". But this was 1974 and there on the floor were dream cars enough to convince any car lover he had died and gone to heaven. There was a silver BMW 3.0 CS Coupe and, crouching next to it, an exotic yellow Ferrari Dino.

The salesman – a likable young chap – was easily convinced that I might buy a Ferrari or a BMW or, who knows, maybe both. What did he know? What did he care? We were both going to have one helluva' spring day "test driving" the cars. We did. I knew little about Ferraris, but we didn't confine our testing to the comparatively meek Dino V-6, sweet as it was. Oh no; we took on the big Ferraris; the 12-cylinder jobs. The dealer had a variety of used ones he would love to unload. Had I known Ferraris and could I have peered into the future, I might have realized that one or more of those big, old late-sixties-early-seventies Ferraris would some day make their owner millionaire-rich. In fact, had I bought the Dino as I almost did, I might have sold it later for a hundred grand or more; before the Ferrari market took its dive.

"Car buying should be an adventure, an event," I said to the young salesman who was having every bit as much fun as I was. By late afternoon, I sensed that I had pushed this game about as far as it could be pushed. We returned to the show floor. I took one more long, longing look at the yellow Ferrari…and bought the silver BMW. It wasn't the difference in price but the difference in practical. The Ferrari had sex; it didn't have space for the tools of my trade, much less family or friends.

I hated practical. Still, the BMW CS Coupe wasn't a bad consolation prize. I pointed the Bimmer westward and headed out into Chicago's goin' home traffic.

Cargoyles: hatched to spoil the fun of driving

The car was too beautiful; the day was too beautiful; the moment was too beautiful to think about "that other car", the yellow Ferrari. I determined to sit back and savor the euphoria of driving one of the finest automobiles ever to come out of Bavaria – or anywhere else in the world for that matter.

I couldn't know that I would still be driving this marvelous machine decades later. I didn't want to know that the "Gotcha" Cargoyle would still be menacing motorists and feeding on their fines. It would have been inconceivable – even to my cynical mind – that this Cargoyle would become only one of a tribe of Cargoyles, all of them hatched to spoil the fun of driving.

My immediate attention was directed to the traffic flow heading west out of Chicago. It was thinning out. I pointed the sensuous snout of the silver BMW off on a back road; the first leg of my pre-planned escape route. Between the

Heavy metal

BMW dealership and my St. Paul home, there was an intricate interlinking of back roads; some 400 miles of them. They twisted, they turned, they swooped into tiny hamlets; sometimes they dissected a farm yard; home on one side of the road; barn on the other side.

"It must be hell at milking time," I mused as I cruised through one such farm yard. The farm kid in me – the one that never grew up – commanded me to slow down. I did. I know about farmers, about farm kids, about their livestock and their pets. No dude in a high powered car has any right to endanger them. There are right times and there are right roads for mashing the gas pedal a bit.

This was not the time or place.

As I see it, there will always be dimwit drivers. They'll damn well drive whatever way they please; and screw what happens to you, me or anyone else who might get in their way…or in their car. These jerks are not just involved in more accidents than everybody else; they cause them. Careless driving remains the leading cause of accidents; speed only a 5% factor. Better control of who gets – and gets to keep – a driver's license might help; so would strict penalties for dimwit driving. A national speed limit will not and cannot. It only hamstrings the daily lives of sensible people who have work to do and places to go.

Hell, I've driven twice, three times the 55 speed limit – the higher speeds on race tracks or deserted roads – but always with great concern for the safety of my fellow humans and other living creatures. Put me on icy roads, congested roads and the like; I'm the one going slower than the proverbial little old lady.

Driving at any speed – but particularly fast – demands that you have some idea of what it is you are about. Your car probably weighs in at nearly two tons. Heavy metal. Hit something, and your car stops, but you become the multi-ton projectile still traveling at your car's previous speed. Even our aforementioned little old lady has the power to bend a steering wheel to the dash or catapult through a windshield. Messy! In my news reporter days, I photographed and "covered" enough gory accident scenes to last a lifetime.

Driving is serious business. I'm no expert, but I work at it. I know how engines, fuel systems, electrical systems, clutches, transmissions, drive shafts, brakes, tires and most all the "mechanics" work and why. It helps me stay on course and stay alive. I've taken defensive driving courses, race track driver training and more. I learn everything I can about cars and the art of driving them.

Driving is not an activity for dimwits. Telling Americans how and how fast to drive is not for bureaucratic nitwits; nitwits like the "Gotcha" Gang in Washington who came up with the Uniform National Speed Limit law. In the West and Midwest – my country – we govern ourselves mostly by common sense. "Horse sense" as my horse-loving dad used to say,

The horses in my BMW, reined in as I threaded my way through occupied territory, were anxious to be let out. Just ahead lay get-up-and-go land; a road that seemed to rise and fall and twist its way to infinity. Free wheelin' land!

The land of the free and the brave was, I knew, rapidly becoming the Nanny Nation. Before turning 30, I had already served in both World Wall II and Korea. I would be damned if I was now going to let mindless Auto Immune federal rule-makers tell me how to drive my car.

Especially, they would not diminish the euphoria of this day: my maiden voyage in this elegant BMW coupe. The brand-newness of it enveloped my senses. Someone, I thought, should blend the smell of new leather into an exotic perfume for women. Car guys wouldn't be able to resist.

The silver Bimmer was now in open, deserted straight-a-way. Instinctively, I planted my right foot down, and the big straight six came to life with a muted growl. In seconds, we had doubled the sacred 55-mile speed limit and the needle was still climbing. The engine sounds, the smells and the serenity of the open country were making their way from my brain to my soul. How could anyone not love cars? Why could they not comprehend the immeasurable pleasure of driving; real participatory driving; not just steering? Why in God's name would they pass a dumb law that would have everyone poking along at speeds slower than grandpa used to drive?

Get-up-and-go-land

Of course, I knew the official answer: "we're saving fuel that those nasty Arabs are threatening to cut off. It's the patriotic thing to do.

"Bull shit!", I shouted to the world.

Then I saw it!

It's hard to put into words the thrill of an occasional burst of speed at the wheel of a car that was bred for speed. Rich Ceppos, writing for Automobile magazine, nails it better than just about anyone as he tells of driving a 456GT Ferrari flat out – 186 mph, that is – in Italy. Says he:

"A good dose of speed is like spring cleaning for the soul…after you come back to earth from a foray to the far side of the speedometer…the sky is bluer, the steaks are tastier, and the women are prettier."

Rich wrote these words some 20 years after my 3.0 maiden voyage, but then, as today, I know exactly what he means.

Reluctantly, I had to re-enter the freeway just long enough to reach the next exit and the final l00 miles of twisty two-laners that would lead me home. I eased off the gas and settled in to tolerate the next ten miles of freeway boredom.

Then I saw it!

There, smack dab in the center of the Bimmer's expansive rear window were the all-too-familiar flashing, pulsating red lights. The "Gotcha" enforcer had me cold.

"Sixty eight miles an hour!" the trooper said with a scathing solemnity that might have been more appropriate for pronouncements like, "I'm arresting you for treason," or "I'll take that gun now."

The $70 "bond" – which the judge suggested I would be wise to forfeit – might have been less painful were it not for the 30-mile journey to the nearest constable. Townsfolk on their front porches must have felt safer in their beds that night as they watched the trooper parade me through streets that lead to the court house. The trooper, of course, couldn't be blamed. This was the new

Near sensory overload

federal policy to control America's lawless, gas-wasting drivers. Failure to vigorously enforce meant cuts in federal highway funds, and maybe the trooper's job, too, for all I knew. Besides it was tax revenue for this little Wisconsin town; revenue that wouldn't offend the townsfolk and somehow seemed to be "promoting public safety."

Chastened and poorer, I headed back out of town, trying not to meet the accusing stares of the local citizenry.

Surprisingly, the hum of the big BMW power plant had a therapeutic effect, soothing the rage that had been building in me since my humbling arrest. I concentrated on enjoying the final miles into St.Paul. My attention, nonetheless, was never far from the rear view mirror. It was a driving position I would perfect in the years to come.

Mimi – my wife whose beauty is always enhanced by her tolerance for my auto addiction – greeted me as I swung triumphantly into our driveway. Later, we cruised the neighborhood and I turned on the stereo for the first time. Mimi, I knew, didn't share my appreciation of the "symphony of cylinders". This is music only perceptible to the AED. Her perfume was overwhelmed by the aroma of leather upholstery. Heaven! The woman you love in the car you love; a spring breeze wafting through open windows; stars visible through the sun roof.

With this near sensory overload of pleasure, I was still troubled by a nagging suspicion brought on by my arrest; something I would confess at a more appropriate time. Somewhere in America – maybe many somewheres – the Auto Immune forces were immersed in pleasure too. I could almost hear their chant:

> "Fifty five; stay alive. Fifty five wherever you drive."

I could even picture their parties. One Auto Immune dolt approaches another and their wine glasses clink. Through tears of joy they proclaim…

"Think of it! Now we can tell everyone how fast to drive. We'll have millions – maybe even billions – to spend!"

Cathedral windows for your garage?

Then again, maybe I was just brooding over my "Gotcha" encounter. It was time to put the "silver bomb" away for the night.

Next morning – even earlier than my usual "morning person" start – I slipped into the side door of my garage. Reverently, transfixed by the moment, I drank in the beauty of this magnificent machine. Sunlight swathed its seductive shape.

When car guys take over the world, I thought, we will build garages with cathedral windows worthy of the vehicles inside.

At last able to move, I slid behind the wheel, inhaling the intoxicating leather aroma; awed by the craftsmanship that must have gone into those blue leather seats. There was even a leather encased stick; a baton with which to conduct the symphony of sounds and sensations to come.

"These Bavarians, they know how to build cars," I announced to myself, inserting the key into the ignition with a flourish and thrust befitting the occasion. This, after all, was a milestone morning and a religious rite; not just the start of another work day. In seconds I would hear a whirring starter motor and the engine would come alive, making me more alive in the process.

I might just take the long way to work. Sure, I had driven 400 miles yesterday, but my AED addiction craves constant fulfillment. Is sex any less satisfying today just because you had sex yesterday? One thing for sure, the "don't-dare-go-over-55" crowd could go straight to hell. This baby was built to move!

Even the key was a work of engineering art. Not stamped out of some wimpy sheet metal; this was no-nonsense, fat, heft-in-your-hand steel. Both sides had been drilled with indentations varying in depth by only thousands of an inch. Let some crummy thief try to copy this key. I twisted it in the ignition with an I'm-in-charge-here authority.

Nothing! No whir of the starter. Nothing!

I tried again and again. Silence; silence broken only by my screams of obscenity and alternate pleading with the Almighty. My world; my world that been filled with such excitement and anticipation only moments before had deteriorated to abject helplessness and frustration. I fumed, cursed, checked the battery and electrical connections, cursed some more. Everything I had ever learned from years of not only tinkering with cars but sometimes completely overhauling them was brought to bear on the problem.

There were no answers; only a sulking silver beauty that refused to respond.

When the Chicago dealership opened for business – finally! – the first sleepy mechanic to answer the phone was hit by an irate customer exploding in his ear.

"The seat belts have to be fastened before she'll start," the mechanic explained with more patience and courtesy than I deserved.

"What the hell are you telling me?" I yelled.

"Don't blame me; its the new law," the mechanic shot back. "Unless your seat belts are buckled, she ain't gonna' start and that's all there is to it."

"Damn liberals!" I screamed, "They want to control my whole life."

What in hell would they think of next? It was a rhetorical question. Still, if liberal headquarters had been listening in, their answer would have been a resounding "plenty."

Ironically, I would have discovered the trick seat belts earlier in my BMW ownership but for the fact that I was such a devout seat belt believer that my belts are almost always fastened before I start any car. I didn't need any snot-nosed control freak in Washington rigging my car. Twice in 24 hours, the long arm of federal life-control had grabbed me by the scruff of the neck to tell me how to operate my new BMW. I didn't take kindly to that.

Snot-nosed control freaks

An idea whose time had not come... yet

What really steamed me is that they were harassing a guy who had been using seat belts since the 1950's when seat belts were an install-it-yourself after market purchase. I had crunched many a knuckle in the seat belt installation process.

Way back in 1963, in fact, I had launched a one-man crusade to get all Americans to buy and use seat belts as religiously as the Kamstra family did. My idea was simple; required no federal funding or fumbling around with ignition systems.

At the heart of the concept was a $10,000 life insurance policy – free to all takers. Install and use seat belts and if they didn't save your life in a crash, your surviving loved ones would at least have an additional $10,000 in your estate. The insurance provider would accept minimal risk – because seat belts really do save lives – and the company would get, in turn, millions of prospect names and addresses of those accepting the free policies.

The seat belt maker, on the other hand, would, in effect, be demonstrating so much confidence in his product that it was backed by free insurance. It was, in my humble opinion, such a brilliant concept that soon millions would be enhancing their chances of surviving car crashes. Not incidentally, of course, I would soon be enhancing my personal fortunes as well.

It didn't happen.

I spent months – not to mention more of the family budget than I could justify – calling on major insurance companies and seat belt manufacturers. To maximize chances of success, I presented only to presidents and C.E.O.'s. My methods of reaching these high level audiences must remain a trade secret, but I managed to pull it off. No jealous underling was going to kill my concept before it had a chance to live. In every instance, the interest was present but never enough to propel a program launch.

It was an idea whose time had not come…yet. Decades later, General Motors announced its own version of the insurance-for-seat-belt wearers program. I wrote their president; he ignored me; I wasn't surprised.

And here it was, 1974, and some damn bureaucrat was wiring my BMW to force me to buckle up. I drove – the long way – to work that morning. Driving is good thinking time. Life is like driving, I thought; there is always a new challenge just over the hill.

■ ■ ■

Bimmer Meets Brainerd Race Track. Porsche Club members prepare for a weekend of competitive driving. During the author's brief "racing career", his 911E Porsche Targa was "vehicle of choice". Here, his gleaming new BMW 3.0 CS Coupe awaits its turn for some "unofficial" track time. No racing, understand; just see how the coupe would perform. Some race-prepared 3.0's do very well in competition. This just-for-fun run was just that, fun. Used to running low slung Porsches, the author found himself ducking as the 3.0 screamed under pedestrian bridges. Today – more than a quarter century later – this 3.0 is still high on his list of fun cars.

CHAPTER 25

Up Your Tailpipe;
The Smell Of Auto Oblivion

The Auto Restriction Group (ARG)

The lines weren't unreasonably long when I swung my aging Porsche into the neighborhood Emissions Testing Center but the wait was. Plenty of time for growing rage. Time, too, for rumination on how this latest federal tax scam was foisted off on gullible motorists, convinced it was all for the good of Mother Earth.

I try to imagine how it all came about.

Maybe some zealot in the Environmental Protection Agency awoke one morning, looked out the window at all the Washington commuters and screamed, "They're driving to work like nothing is wrong. My God, don't they realize their cars are killing the planet! They're not car pooling. Those reckless ass holes are probably going over 55 miles and hour too. Why can't they see what they're doing to our beautiful world!"

The zealot is bewildered. Even back in the sixties – as a non-inhaling student – the environmental warnings were looming. Profound, scientific-sounding books predicted an auto-induced Armageddon. Earth Day was invented. Worldwide save-the-planet conferences were staged, demanding that American taxpayers pay billions to help all nations fight environmental sins.

Was it all coming to this? People just driving to work in their cars; going about their lives; not willing to get involved in the great Earth Mother Movement. Heaven help us! There had to be a way; a way to slap lethargic citizens – particularly those damn car nuts – along side the head. Make them wake up and start worrying.

Environmental activists, inspired by their beloved leader, Al Gore, know that cars will bring an end to all life on this planet. Too late, motorists will panic. They will choke every highway and escape route in a vain effort to escape; to find just one more lungful of air to breath. Instead, they will, of course, only be hastening their own horrible, gasping deaths as their cars consume the last oxygen on earth.

Maybe someone in Washington called an emergency meeting of the Auto Restriction Group (ARG). However it came about, the solution was nothing short of pure political genius. With one stroke of the lawmaker's pen, unwary U.S. motorists would not only be reminded of their ecological sins…they would be forced to continually remind themselves. Equally ingenious – albeit standard federal operating procedure – every motorist would pay a fee (tax) to have a government agency "test" his car's exhaust. Like docile lambs, each motorist would fall in line for the annual testing ritual.

Just as I was doing as I pondered this latest government fraud.

■ ■ ■

Behold, another Cargoyle is born. The Cargoyle, "Snifferous", a vile creature, would sustain his life by inhaling your car's exhaust. "Snifferous" was to become a vampire for the Twenty First Century.

The Cargoyle, Snifferous: vampire for the 21st century

The Tailpipe Air Purity (TAP) act would forever extract cash from each motorist as he or she waited nervously in line for annual emissions testing ritual. Our benevolent government had found a way to force everyone to worry about the coming environmental Dooms Day. Indeed, everyone worried. They wondered how much oxygen was really left in the world. Would it ultimately be rationed? Would the rich get more oxygen than poor people? Would nations go to war over breathing rights?

"The guy in front of me; his exhaust is coming right into my car! I'm going to die! I'm going to die! I'll never even know whether my car would have passed the test!"

Some panicked. Some hyperventilated. Some fled in terror, vowing to hide out in the mountains…or maybe even South Dakota.

Almost everyone passes the test, of course. Everyone worries. Everyone pays. The TAP Act is working beautifully. No one – least of all the testers – knows exactly how the test standards were established or who made the rules. Motorists – so enormously relieved to pass the test and be permitted to keep on driving – don't really care.

Snifferous

Hold still. Snifferous wants to check your car again. Beware. His standards – and his fees – are getting higher and higher. He's the Cargoyle with clout; official sniffer, tester and score keeper for a nation obsessed with the purity of your car's exhaust. So what if your car's breath may now be more pure than your own. Snifferous has a job to do. Besides, he just doesn't like you and that offensive machine you drive. With each examination he gives you, he hopes to prick your environmental conscience. He knows he will pick your pocket. Billions in new revenues, new EPA careers. The federal trough is bottomless; life is good. May Snifferous endure through the ages.

■ ■ ■

He'll poke and probe about your vehicle. The sweat builds up then starts to trickle. The "FAIL" stamp spells complete disgrace. "Start walking now and leave this place!"

The Tailpipe Air Purity Act. (TAP)

The TAP Act. An act of political genius. Tap the mind; tap the money.

State governments bought land; built test centers on the land; filled the centers with expensive, high tech testing equipment. Center operators – mostly teenagers -- assumed an air of earth-saving holiness as they bestowed each "recertification" certificate on cowering car owners. Drivers are being properly humbled before their omnipotent, all-seeing, all-caring government. Young people are learning: government is good; citizens are bad; bad, evil polluters who must be controlled lest they destroy their own environment.

Government control of the barbarian motorist is tightening. Don't dare drive fast or we'll fine (tax) you. Don't burn too much gas-per-mile or we'll penalize (tax) you. Don't pay more for your car than we think is sensible or we'll "luxury" tax you. And now, let us put our testing equipment up your tailpipe. If you fail, we'll tax you; if you pass, we'll still tax you.

Soon – no matter how many pollution tests your car passes – your benign government caretakers will mandate electric cars. Some are at your friendly neighborhood car dealer already.

■ ■ ■

Finally, it's my turn. The young lady inserts the testing rod up the rumbling exhaust of my Porsche. Minutes later, she smiles and announces, "you passed."

I don't return the smile. My Porsche and I have just been violated.

■ ■ ■

Minnesota Imports A Classic London-To-Brighton Run And Thousands Turn Out

Once upon a time (1890), cars could not drive on England's roads unless a man walked ahead waving a red flag. The flag warned horse-drawn carriages that one of those damnable "horseless carriages" was about. When the law was repealed (1896) AED suffering Brits celebrated with an auto run from London to Brighton. The 57-mile endurance event – run every year since – has become the world's largest spectator event with 2 million celebrating motoring freedom.

Minnesota's car buffs, brooding during 6 months of winter, decided one day in 1987 to import the classic run. Their version: 120 miles from rural Minnesota's New London to New Brighton, a Twin Cities suburb. As in the England event, participants dress in costume and just generally have a good time. Matter of fact, some participants ship their cars from England to be part of the event, which includes a smorgasbord of Minnesota hospitality along the route.

"You might approach 30 miles per hour at times... if the mechanics are just right" says Jim Forest, an avid fan and one of the event's organizers. "But the average speed will be about 20." There are the picnic lunches and the cheering crowds along the way. Speed is not what it is all about.

"We have been forced to the side of the road by the rush of technology. No longer can we safely venture into today's highway traffic", laments Forest. "This event stakes out our claim to a portion of the modern transportation system. We refuse to let our cars be relegated to museums."

Eligibility rules are strict. No cars newer than 1908. Exception: 1 or 2 cylinder vehicles up to 1915 vintage. Steam, electric or gas driven. Bikes or motorcycles too. First 100 entries accepted.

Jim's car is a 1910 Brush roadster. One cylinder. He knows what "It's Okay To Love Your Car" means. "My Brush has a spirit and personality distinct from any other car, even its contemporaries." No controlled environment as you travel. No windshield. Open the throttle and the wind shrieks through your hair as the countryside totters past. One cylinder is all you need and the transmission has one gear to get started and another for all other conditions.

You can cheer Jim Forest and all the other New London-to-New Brighton competitors every August in Minnesota. Don't come late; winter may come early this year.

Jim and Helen Forest cross the Finish Line in their beloved 1910 Brush Roadster.

CHAPTER 26

"STEEROIDS" LAUNCH
THE MICROCHIP MILLENNIUM

Microchips are replacing minds

It hurts me to write this. Yet, I suppose it was inevitable; the relentless force of change and all that. Fact is, they're not making cars that require real, participate-in-the-process drivers anymore; and they're not raising kids who really care.

What happened to this new generation of motorists; one cannot call them "drivers"? They should be lamenting or even outraged by the fact that microchips are replacing minds in the operation of their cars. They have been automotively lobotomized. That's what happened to them. We have bred a nation – a world – of "Steeroids"; weenie-like creatures capable only of steering their homogenized, jelly-bean-shaped vehicles from one computer store to another. These geeks would rather play with computers than cars; and cars are obliging them by fast becoming mere computers on wheels.

This development can be as lethal as it is lamentable. Steeroids steer and they stomp. Stomp on the gas. Stomp on the brakes. Even the elementary mind-body coordination demanded of this steer-and-stomp sequence is too much for many Steeroids. Coming from schools that stress self esteem, "feel-good" confidence over competence – 300 horsepower engines blazing – these swooping darting Steeroids daily terrorize other motorists .

Futurists probably saw it all coming. I must confess, I didn't. The press – with the detachment of the Auto Immune – has noted it. They're not alarmed about this auto-emasculation of our youth; just noting that it is taking place.

The *Wall Street Journal,* in a recent interview regarding the latest advance in personal computers, reports that "the world has moved from the age of machines to the age of information." A car dealer is quoted as finding young guys more interested in new computer software than a hard-charging sports car. This in spite of the fact that car makers are appealing to the youth market with Rambo names, spoilers, air scoops, swoopy style and cop-bating colors.

Evidence of this mass automotive lobotomy is not hard to find. I was with a friend of mine the day he proudly presented his 16-year-old son with his very own car. His son, Jeff, assumed that air of know-it-all nonchalance that only teen age sons can pull off. Nonetheless, he followed Dad out to the driveway. There it was: Jeff's very first car. It wasn't new – a vintage 1984 Subaru station wagon – and it didn't really shine in spite of Dad's clandestine polishing efforts. All that didn't matter; perception was a everything at this milestone moment in father-son relationships. A car, down through the decades, has always been one of the basic male gender urges. A rite of passage. Wheels! Wheels, in turn, facilitate satisfaction of other male urges. Dad hadn't thought that far ahead; Dad's seldom do.

A guy thing

"Wow!" It was about as profound as Jeff could be at that moment; but his nonchalance was breaking down. He was definitely impressed.

"She's a beauty and she's all yours."

"Thanks, Dad."

It wasn't really a beauty; it was a little shabby in fact. Still, beauty is in the eye of the beholder during male bonding. A guy thing. Not unlike that plain Jane down the bar whose beauty is enhanced with each succeeding sip of your Scotch.

Jeff was by now downright intoxicated with the euphoria of the moment. Down on his haunches, he bounced around the car, checking it out like a Grand Prix contender readying for a race.

Then came the climactic moment. Jeff slid his 128-pound frame behind the wheel. Command center. Look out, world, here I come! Suddenly, the joy was gone. Even before Jeff spoke, Dad knew something was terribly wrong.

"Dad! Dad! This thing has a got a stick shift!" He couldn't have been more repulsed had he discovered an over-ripe corpse in the passenger seat.

It could only have happened on the eve of the twenty first century; The Microchip Millennium, ushering in a generation of youth disinterested in the plebeian inconveniences of clutches, gear shifting and the like. Dad should have known. He should have remembered that day when Jeff came home from first grade, all excited about being chosen to lead computer training classes.

Twenty first century youth does not memorize multiplication tables.

"That's why we have calculators."

Twenty first century youth does not shift cars.

"That's why God gave us computers."

■ ■ ■

"I'll take over now, you drone"

Dad – his 50th birthday closing in – had to look no further for clues to Jeff's behavior than his own garage. When was the last time a stick shift machine occupied one of the stalls? Had he thought about it, he probably couldn't remember. His present car – the one with the melted jelly bean shape like most every other car – certainly had no stick to shift. It did have a macho cockpit that would have been the envy of any World War II fighter pilot. The heated bucket seat – with adjustable lumbar support and eight-way, full-memory positioning – contained and pampered his spreading bulk.

A gazillion micro-controllers were connected by more than a mile of wires crammed into the doors and dash of Dad's sleek new machine. They energized an array of impressive gizmos that faced him and wrapped around him as he looked over the padded, air-bag-loaded steering wheel. Tiny, pimple-sized lights were everywhere: red ones, green ones, blue ones. There were L.E.D. readouts and a full message center. It was an ergonomic engineer's work of art. Dad – his male hormones stimulated by the array of controls within his reach – would switch "ignition on" and simultaneously, instinctively the fingers on his right hand tensed awaiting the next critical command.

There weren't any.

If you listened, you could almost hear the "Gigatroll" Cargoyle (see next pages) saying, "I'll take over now, you drone."

Dad tried to find something for his mission-tensed fingers to do. Cabin temp: no that's set year around at 72. Stereo station: pre-set many months ago. Message center: all dark, meaning "all systems okay and keep your damn hands off. I'll tell you if there is anything you need to know. You may be miles from nowhere and it'll probably be too late to do anything about it, but I'll let you know if there's trouble."

Push that big, leather encased, phallic-suggestive protrusion in the center console to "drive" and that's it for you, Dad. Everything else will be done for you. A chip will "feather" the brakes so you don't skid; another will – in fractions of a second – alternate power to each wheel so you can get going in snow or ice. But, what the hell, you still get to steer the thing. Steeroid!

With all that, should Dad have really wondered about his son's aversion to manual shifting?

■ ■ ■

Participatory driving

So there they were, this Auto Immune father-son team, coming to grips with evolutional reality. Citizens of the coming Microchip Millennium, unaware of and unconcerned with the sociological significance of their brief exchange. Dad, while he might not want to admit it, probably was not much for participatory driving himself. Son, Jeff, had never been exposed to it and had no interest in starting now. Pity.

So just what the hell is "participatory driving" anyway? It's a philosophy, a gut feeling, a relationship with things mechanical; especially, it involves you and the internal combustion engine that moves you. If you are one of the Auto Immune majority, chances are you will never understand, or even give a damn. Yet there is hope. Maybe your DNA actually does contain the Auto Erotic Gene but you've somehow suppressed it. Never let it advance to full blown AED. Never even heard of participatory driving. Let me explain how it functions.

First, you hit the starter. Feel the engine come to life. You should feel it more than hear it. Sound deadening insulation makes hearing an engine increasingly difficult. If you can feel the engine – if the throb of the engine seems to synchronize with the beat of your heart – then there is hope for you. You may actually possess the rare Auto Erotic Gene. You could become emotionally involved with your car; a hopeless-but-happy AED addict. Your life could be far richer than it is now.

Gigatroll

1 The Gigatroll just wants you to take it easy while he takes control of your car. Why should anyone be bothered with such mundane drudgery anyway? You just steer the thing. That's it; turn it to the right or turn it to the left. Oh, and keep it under 55. Gear shifting? Gear selection? Where have you been? Gigatroll relieved mankind of that ridiculous routine years ago; probably while your parents were still trying to teach you to say, "car car." Gigatroll will shift for you; decide when to turn your headlights on or off; shut down your engine if you drive too fast; screech at you if your parallel parking needs work. There's even better times ahead: "Smart Roads"; Gigatroll's ultimate achievement wherein you become totally unnecessary. With "Smart Roads", you just lock on and lay back while Gigatroll's master computer drives your car and thousands of others at the same time. Gigatroll will alert you when you have reached your destination. Who needs driving?

■ ■ ■

Driving bores you to your soul?
Just give the task to Gigatroll.
Let him control right from the start.
That leaves you free to swoop and dart.

Warming to your passionate command

Other steps in the foreplay of auto eroticism may never again be available to you; but let me tell you "how it was." Dashboards were once adorned with real gauges. You could actually see engine oil pressure build; be comforted as another gauge told you that a generator was already starting to recharge your battery from the drain of starting the engine. The needle on the water temperature gauge would slowly rise as the engine warmed. And you knew that if the needle rose too high, all was not right with the car you loved. Sometimes, there was a gauge to tell you oil temperature, too. You could monitor the engines revolutions-per-minute – RPM's – as you stroked the gas pedal with your toe.

The whole, complex, wonderful system was responding, warming to your passionate command!

Finally, you had but to depress the clutch – there were clutches then – select a gear and begin the most serious, sensuous interplay of all. This interplay – of machine and man being thrust into motion – is primal; probably since humans first felt the sheer joy of speed on foot or on horseback.

Attaining driving age on the open prairies of the Midwest, I was blessed with limitless space in which to hone my driving skills at speeds limited only by my courage and the capabilities of my car. Speed, however, was not a basic requirement for a satisfying life of AED addiction.

One's soul-satisfying experience could be multiplied many times over by a basic understanding of what was happening under the hood and in all recesses and extremities of the vehicle under your control. It was multiplied again if you actually had hands-on experience with the car's mechanical innards.

Farm life – farmers usually fix their own stuff – was the elementary stage of my mechanical learning. It was advanced further in my money-strapped teen years when fix-it-yourself was the only option. The Navy was my "grad school" where I learned how to dismantle engines, rebuild them and reassemble them. My teachers knew all they needed to know about student motivation.

"Get that damn engine running, sailor, or it'll be your sorry ass! And I mean right now! "

I don't recall ever having to ask him to clarify the order. He was dead right, of course. Mechanical ineptitude on my part could well have been my ass, the skipper's ass and the behinds of everyone else aboard that LSM.

That was then; this is now. I lament the passing of the "Participatory Driving Era". Except for the AED addicted enthusiasts, most motorists will never again know about – much less care about – truly participating in the art of operating an internal combustion-powered vehicle.

Intellectually, I understand why it had to happen; emotionally, I don't. Maybe this is how my late and strong willed father felt as he experienced the end of the horse era.

■ ■ ■

As I struggle to find perspective in this final chapter, I ultimately realize that these are the best of times for any and all motorists everywhere. There is a delicious array of cars for any taste or no taste at all. For the Auto Immune Steeroid, most vehicles offer "just-get-in-and-drive" shiftless simplicity. This is true whether the vehicle is a go-anywhere SUV, a pickup truck, a 400 horsepower super car or a just a typical rent-a-car sedan. Even the once-macho marques like Ferrari, Porsche, BMW offer slush box models for Steeroids. Hence this blasphemous ad headline by BMW:

"A STICK IS NO LONGER REQUIRED TO STIR YOUR SOUL"

"Just get in and drive"

Auto Erotic Dependency addiction is timeless

Ecology paranoids have not been left out. Electric cars are showing up in dealer show rooms. There is even a federal tax allowance for those who drive them. The worry for all other motorists is that our government – probably under the Gore administration – may ultimately outlaw internal combustion engines and force us all into electric cars, ride sharing or mass transit.

Enthusiasts, meanwhile, have limitless options. The classics collector can track down cars that date back anywhere in the spectrum of the last 100-plus years of auto manufacture. Not incidentally, car buffs and non-buffs alike should say thanks to the thousands of collectors who lavish so much time and money keeping our automotive heritage alive. Every car lover – whether AED afflicted or not – can see these wonderfully restored cars of almost every make, model or age. Many are for sale; but do require participatory drivers.

I have preserved my "participation cars" from the sixties, seventies and eighties. They are preserved not for any collector value, but because they played a part in this "auto autobiography" and deserve an honored place in the Kamstra family. Would that I could have kept my cars of the forties and fifties, but poverty prevented it.

One of the joys of AED addiction is that it is timeless. Enjoy today by driving whenever and wherever you can. Do it on your own. Get involved in one or more car clubs that abound with interesting people and car-related, fun activities. Nobody has discovered the secret of perpetual youth, but car people come the closest to it.

The new automotive generation is largely unconcerned; accepting their role as Steeroids. Many are eagerly awaiting computer-controlled "smart roads" which will eliminate the need for any kind of participation by drivers.

Among this eager group is the younger generation that have taken the reins at the agency that bears my name. This agency, specializing in "high tech" clients worldwide, has been at once my pipeline to the world of technology as well as a first-hand "observation clinic" of computer literate men and women.

The Kamstra agency has supported my auto addiction since l963 when the agency was just me, operating largely out of the tiny trunk of my 356B Porsche. Today, the multi-acre Kamstra Center headquarters includes space for my beloved cars. These vehicles I understand far better than I do computers.

As this book is about to enter the publishing process, I am planning still another back roads tour of America with Mimi, my wife and navigator. We'll be wearing our "Carmudgeon" shirts, designating our charter membership in my new club for "seasoned" car nuts.

■ ■ ■

Epilogue

Driving Enriches Life
Even If You Don't Dig Cars

The Kamstra agency name now lives on as Bozell Kamstra, incorporated into the operation of one of the world's largest advertising agencies. This perpetuation of my life's work is, of course, most satisfying. Deeper reflection is in order, however. How did this improbable scenario come about anyway? This book attempts to answer that question, albeit from a car nut's point of view. It chronicles poverty-to-riches success but yet it's not still another "How To Succeed" manual. Besides a reassurance about your love of cars, is there something of value you, the reader, can take from it?

Maybe there is. An incident that occurred not long before I sold the agency illustrated – quite by happenstance – one of my "success secrets". It had to do with a visitor to the new "Kamstra Center".

She was a pretty young woman. Her tailored business suit, muted but warm red, set off her dark tresses. Tresses that could have been featured in any shampoo commercial. I joined an assortment of Kamstra execs eagerly awaiting her. From the moment of her arrival, we fawned over her, proudly toured our new headquarters, served her iced tea. She was, after all, a journalist representing a leading American "ad biz" publication.

Our PR people had arranged for her visit to follow the early Friday adjournment of a two-day ad industry conference she had been attending in our Twin Cities.

"I thought it would never end", she sighed as she sank into one of our conference room chairs. "I'll be glad to catch my flight back home."

We sympathized. Leaned on every word.

She went on about some jerk who had been hitting on her all during the incoming flight. She hoped there would be no repeat of this problem going home. Even at my age, I could see why it might happen.

We sympathized; poured more tea.

"I was a journalist myself," I volunteered awkwardly, hoping it might trigger a beginning of the much-anticipated interview. My younger male colleagues were anxious to expound on our growth and the state-of-the-art features of Kamstra Center. I suspect, though, that they found it satisfying just to exchange pleasantries with such a fetching female.

I, too, wanted to talk Kamstra growth; maybe contribute insights that only a founder could provide. Immodestly, I envisioned taking maybe a bit more than my share of the credit for what a few decades of dedication had brought about. The tree-shaded Kamstra Center campus stood as undeniable evidence of our progress, of course, but maybe Ms. Reporter would delve into "the story behind the story".

> "South Dakota Farm Boy Makes Good In Big City,
> Big Time Ad Business"

That sort of thing.

I fed her more "pump priming" story hints. She took no notes, asked no questions. Staffers offered to feed her cookies. She declined, looked at her watch. Her attitude seemed to say, "It's all about me."

"You have beautiful offices here", she said, "It must be a pleasant place to work."

Then she asked for a ride to the airport and left.

No "Kamstra Story" this day.

I was crushed. Then, calmed by my customary Friday night Scotch, I realized that this woman – who may have just been having an off day – was nonetheless dramatizing one of my success secrets.

My "secret" theory: most people aren't willing to work very hard for success. It follows that wherever there is one person unwilling to pay the price of higher achievement, an opportunity awaits for someone else to fill the void. The rule applies anywhere in any field of endeavor. In my opinion, those unwilling to strive number in the millions. You pick your own number. There's room for you to excel and it is never too early or too late to start.

As my former boss and billionaire business tycoon, the late Curt Carlson, always said, "the harder I work, the luckier I get." Were Curt alive today, I am sure he would agree that it is the striving and achieving, not the money alone, that enriches life.

The exceptional performers among today's journalists must cringe at colleagues who are unmotivated or, worse, see their primary mission as fanning the flames of class warfare. They're missing the fun of fulfillment.

I believe one's "psyche" – if we pay attention to it – can enrich our lives too. Webster defines "psyche" as our "mental or psychological structure…especially as a motive force." Could there be some connection in our need to drive our cars and the way we drive ourselves? I believe there is. My psyche, for instance, is only satisfied by unrestricted driving, whether piloting an interesting car or an exciting entrepreneurial venture.

Long before I gave much thought to my psyche, it was probably functioning as my "motive force". The audacity, for instance, of starting Kamstra Communications and attracting Fortune 500 clients. Who in hell does this high school drop-out think he is? Answer: he's a guy who didn't realize "it can't be done." It could be done and it was; enriching my life beyond my favorite fantasies.

Even if cars don't interest you, consider becoming a driver if you think your psyche might so motivate you. It beats most other life strategies whether you strike out on your own or not. On your own, you probably will start with more credentials and cash than I had, but you will still be swimming up stream. We live in a nation now geared to the insecure and the dependent. Government at all levels discourages individual driving; cars or entrepreneurial ventures. Their "compassion" is funded by confiscating cash from achievers, then redistributing it to those less driven. These road blocks will enrage you but you can still succeed.

"Find a need and fill it." That was my guiding principle. The Twin Cities was already overpopulated with established agencies feeding on ad income. Kamstra Communications concentrated on other, neglected communications opportunities, especially sales promotion. Before long, clients – even some "famous-name companies" – began to seek out our little shop. We were the burr under big agency saddles and a drain on their budgets. Sadistic fun.

We kept growing. I kept the "Prairie Rambler" concept alive. Minimum time at the office; maximum time behind the wheel serving existing clients; seeking new ones.

One of the most ego-wrenching stages in our evolution was my surrender of the creative directorship. Nonetheless, I was still owner/president, calling the shots on agency strategy; taking all the financial risks. One risk was a move to "internationalize" the agency. "Kamstra International" was duly incorporated just outside London.

Not a good gamble. A new agency in a foreign country devours cash; more than I could ever sustain. To cut my losses, I established a joint venture with an existing London agency. This worked. We exploited our "London connection" to attract new business. I shall always remember standing with Mimi in a tiny post office in Marlowe, England, licking stamps and envelopes for a U.S. promotion of our newly-acquired "international status".

In the same year, 1982, we founded "Kamstra Southwest" in Austin, Texas. More agency promotion. More "new horizon" Porsche, BMW driving opportunities between St. Paul and Austin. Once, Mimi spent a month with me in an Austin hotel. I was keeping a promise to a new account; she was serving as gracious "first lady" of Austin's newest ad agency.

Being the driving force behind Kamstra was a seven-days-a-week, dawn-to-late night responsibility. If I was to spend time with Mimi, it would often have to be "company time". London was exciting for her; being abandoned in a hotel room while I made all-day prospecting sorties was not.

Incidentally, when driving in England, beware that most country roads have not been widened or improved since they were built by the Romans centuries ago. An extra coat of paint on your car can be a hazard to you when meeting oncoming traffic.

Owning and "exercising" my cars was my self-reward for the considerable price and pace of success. It was also my favorite therapy to counteract the unrelenting demands of driving my own business as well as that of my clients.

The construction of Kamstra Center was, of course, a milestone in the 34-year evolution of the once basement-based agency. Stone structures nestled among pine trees on a four acre campus, it was a pleasant workplace for all. Outdoor picnic lunches and impromptu meetings were the order of any nice day.

Admiring our new headquarters triggers reminiscence of the early "laundry room" days. It had been a long, arduous but mostly enjoyable run. Now it was time for new frontiers and a new generation of "Kamstra People".

In 1997, Kamstra Communications became "Bozell Kamstra", part of a multi-billion dollar agency empire with 90 offices worldwide. The Bozell Kamstra name would be on the door of a few of them. The "Kamstra Brand" was to be perpetuated.

What's next? My psyche is still a "motive force" as I start a new company, "The Idea Shelf". I will look for interesting cars to drive; swap "car stories" with fellow AED addicts. At almost any age, one can start "thinking old". I will find new ways to sustain – regenerate if necessary – my enthusiasm for life and the opportunities ahead. I'm driven by a line in my motivational film, "Think Higher":

> "The tragedy of life is what dies inside a man while he lives."

Some sage, probably a car guy, wrote that. Translation: "Keep on driving!"

■ ■ ■